A Citizen's Guide to Constitutional Democracy in Botswana

Oagile Bethuel Key Dingake

notionpress.com

INDIA • SINGAPORE • MALAYSIA

ISBN

Hardcase 979-8-90431-927-4
Paperback 979-8-90362-321-1

WE THE PEOPLE: A CITIZEN'S GUIDE TO CONSTITUTIONAL DEMOCRACY IN BOTSWANA

CONTENTS

PREFACE

This book has been written in simple plain English to introduce readers to the idea of a Constitution, republicanism, and the process of reviewing a Constitution. By design, the pages of this booklet are brief. This is meant to facilitate interest in reading the book and absorbing its content faster.

It is hoped that this book will promote and enhance constitutional literacy and an understanding of how government works in a constitutional democracy. Hopefully, this book can be used at an appropriate level within the school system, as well as by members of the public who wish to learn more about Botswana's constitutional framework.

Part One of the book focuses on the foundations of the Constitution of Botswana. It begins by explaining the historical development of the Constitution, showing how Botswana's constitutional system came into being and how it has evolved. It then discusses why societies need government and introduces key ideas such as republican government and constitutional government. These concepts help explain how power is obtained, exercised, and limited in a democratic society.

Part One also explores how government can be organised in ways that prevent the abuse of power. It explains the importance of rules, institutions and checks and balances in ensuring that those in authority act within the law. In addition, it highlights how the Constitution protects fundamental rights and freedoms, and why these protections are essential for human dignity, equality and justice.

Part Two of the book deals with Constitutional Review. It explains that reviewing a constitution involves both process and content, and that these two aspects are equally important. The process refers to how a Constitution is reviewed, including who is involved and how decisions are made. The content refers to what changes are considered and why they may be necessary. Part Two also includes recommendations on how a constitution can be reviewed in the best possible way, with the aim of ensuring legitimacy, public participation and respect for democratic values.

Overall, this book seeks to build a basic but meaningful understanding of the Constitution of Botswana. By increasing constitutional awareness and knowledge, it aims to encourage informed citizenship and active participation in the governance of the country.

– Hon Justice Professor OBK Dingake.
Boroko, NCD, Port Moresby,
Papua New Guinea

PART I

UNDERSTANDING BOTSWANA'S CONSTITUTIONAL IDENTITY

Chapter One

FOUNDATIONS OF THE CONSTITUTION OF BOTSWANA

1.1 INTRODUCTION

Constitutional law sits at an intersection of law and politics. The Constitution is both a legally binding document and a political settlement or compromise reflecting struggles over power, legitimacy and collective identity. That explains why constitution-making or review is inevitably political and a contested process. It reflects and shapes social conflict, history, elite bargains and popular aspirations. The character of our current Constitution is heavily influenced by history, and aspirations for democratic reforms and ongoing struggles over executive power, judicial independence and social justice drive the demand for a comprehensive constitutional review.

To understand where Botswana stands today, and to appreciate why the question of constitutional review has become so urgent, one must first understand where the Constitution came from. The journey to Botswana's independence Constitution was neither sudden nor simple. It unfolded through a series of negotiations and discussions that spanned several years and involved multiple actors, both local and foreign. Understanding this history is essential, for the process by which a constitution is born leaves indelible marks on its character, its strengths, and its blind spots.

1.2 THE HISTORICAL JOURNEY TO INDEPENDENCE

1.2.1 Lancaster House Constitutional Conference (1965)

Botswana's constitutional journey formally began at the Lancaster House Conference in London in 1965, while the country was still the British Protectorate of Bechuanaland. It is important to note that:

- The conference brought together British officials and Bechuanaland leaders, notably the leaders of the political parties then in existence.
- Its main purpose was to design a constitutional framework that would lead to self-government and independence.
- Key principles agreed upon included parliamentary democracy, universal adult suffrage, the rule of law and protection of fundamental human rights.

The Lancaster House Conference was, in many respects, a product of its time. It was a negotiation between colonial administrators and local political elites, conducted in a foreign capital, far removed from the villages and communities where most Batswana lived. The urgency of independence, coupled with the relative stability of the protectorate compared to other African colonies, meant that the discussions were focused on creating a functional framework for self-government rather than on forging a broad-based social compact. The resulting document reflected British constitutional traditions adapted to local circumstances. Still, it did not emerge from the kind of popular consultation that modern democratic theory regards as essential for constitutional legitimacy.

1.2.2 Lobatse Constitutional Talks (1963–1965)

Before and alongside Lancaster House, important constitutional discussions took place in Lobatse.

- These talks involved local political leaders, traditional authorities, and colonial officials.

- They focused on internal issues, such as the structure of government, the role of Dikgosi (chiefs), and the balance between traditional authority and modern democratic institutions.
- A major outcome was the decision to create the House of Chiefs (now Ntlo ya Dikgosi) as an advisory body, ensuring traditional leaders had a voice without undermining elected government.

The Lobatse talks were significant because they provided a space for local actors to shape the constitutional framework. Traditional leaders, who commanded widespread respect in their communities, were able to argue for the preservation of customary institutions within the new democratic order. The creation of the House of Chiefs represented a compromise between those who saw traditional leadership as an obstacle to modern governance and those who viewed it as an essential element of Botswana's cultural identity. This compromise has endured, though the precise role of traditional institutions in a constitutional democracy remains a subject of ongoing debate.

1.2.3 Adoption of the Constitution (1966)

The final Constitution was enacted as the Botswana Independence Constitution, coming into force on 30 September 1966, the day Botswana gained independence.

It established Botswana as a sovereign democratic republic with:

- An executive President
- A unicameral Parliament
- An independent Judiciary
- A Bill of Rights

The Constitution drew heavily from British constitutional traditions but was adapted to Botswana's social and political context.

At independence, Botswana was one of the poorest countries in the world, with limited infrastructure, a small, educated elite and an economy heavily dependent on agriculture and remittances from migrant labour in South African mines. The Constitution provided a framework for stability and gradual development, but it also reflected the limitations of its origins. It was, in many respects, an elite pact rather than a people's charter.

1.3 THE CONSTITUTION AS SUPREME LAW

1.3.1 A Written Constitution

A written Constitution is important for forming and sustaining a nation-State. It is under a written Constitution that the functions of various organs/institutions and functionaries of the State are located. It is also under the Constitution that one can locate the limits of government and its institutions. The Constitution defines the identity of the people and territory that comprise the nation-State and establishes a system of government to govern the collective affairs of the people. It also guarantees the rights of the people.

Lawyers often say that a Constitution is a living document, meaning that it must be relevant to the daily circumstances of the people. A Constitution demands absolute respect from the governors and the governed. A Constitution belongs to the people and does not belong to any single group of people. The people, ideally the creators of the Constitution, delegate whatever power they deem fit to institutions they create. Even judicial power, exercised by judicial officers, is a delegated power. They can make or unmake the Constitution. The politicians do not own the Constitution.

This understanding of the Constitution as belonging to the people, not to the politicians or the government of the day, is fundamental to any meaningful discussion of constitutional review. If the Constitution is understood as a grant of power from the people to their governors, then the people retain the ultimate authority to amend, revise, or replace that grant when it no longer serves their interests or reflects their values.

1.3.2 Supreme Law of the Land

The Constitution is usually the supreme law of the land, and that status is often explicitly stated by the Constitution. Botswana's Constitution is supreme, although the text of the Constitution does not explicitly say so. The courts, after considering the entire scheme of the Constitution, have said so. All other laws, statutes, and regulations are subject to the Constitution, and any law that is inconsistent with the Constitution is invalid to the extent of that inconsistency. Government actions mean Legislative Acts, Executive Acts, Judicial Acts, and/or administrative acts of Government. All arms of Government are under a duty to comply with the Constitution. The superior courts, such as the High Court and Court of Appeal, have the authority to determine constitutional questions.

The supremacy of the Constitution is not merely a technical legal principle; it is the foundation of constitutional governance. It means that no President, no Parliament, no official, and no institution is above the law. All must act within the bounds set by the Constitution, and when they fail to do so, the courts have the authority to intervene. This principle was affirmed and given practical effect in landmark decisions such as *Attorney General v Unity Dow* (1992), where the Court of Appeal struck down legislation that discriminated based on sex, holding that such discrimination violated the Constitution's guarantee of fundamental rights.

1.3.3 Separation of Powers

Another important feature of the Constitution is the idea that the powers of Government must be separated: Separation of Powers. No single authority may exercise key functions of the State alone. Botswana Constitution divides power amongst the three organs of the State: Executive, Legislature and Parliament. The Executive formulates and implements policy, the Legislature passes laws and the Judiciary interprets the law. In Botswana, although the Constitution does not make explicit reference to separation of powers, the courts have pronounced that separation of powers is implicit in the Constitution and characterised it as loose.

The doctrine of separation of powers is a cornerstone of constitutional democracy. It prevents the concentration of power in any single branch and creates a system of mutual oversight and accountability. While Botswana's separation of powers has been described as "loose," the principle remains essential. The Executive administers the country, the Legislature makes the laws, and the Judiciary interprets those laws and ensures that the other branches act constitutionally. When any branch oversteps its bounds, the others have both the authority and the responsibility to push back.

1.4 THE STRUCTURE OF BOTSWANA'S CONSTITUTION

Having examined the historical origins and foundational principles of the Constitution, it is now necessary to understand its basic structure. The Constitution of Botswana, adopted in 1966, is the supreme law of the Republic. It establishes the framework for governance, defines the powers of institutions and guarantees fundamental rights.

- **Supremacy**: No law or action may contradict the Constitution.
- **Flexibility**: While stable, it allows amendments to adapt to changing circumstances.
- **Balance of tradition and modernity**: It incorporates democratic principles alongside respect for customary law.

The recognition of customary courts within the constitutional framework demonstrates Botswana's unique blend of modern governance and traditional practices. This integration is not merely symbolic; it has practical implications for how law is experienced by ordinary citizens, particularly in rural areas where customary courts remain the primary forum for dispute resolution. The Constitution thus operates on multiple levels, speaking simultaneously to the formal institutions of the state and to the lived realities of communities.

1.5 THE UNFINISHED BUSINESS: WHY REVIEW IS NECESSARY

The current Botswana Constitution is time-barred and in urgent need of reform. There is an apparent yearning amongst Batswana to create a modern Constitution that could be a normative statement against authoritarianism. For this aspiration, there is a need for political will and a strong civic culture rooted in the values of transparency, accountability, inclusivity and fairness.

Botswana's Constitution emerged through consultation rather than conflict, moving from Lancaster House negotiations, through local Lobatse discussions, to a carefully crafted independence Constitution in 1966. This foundation has contributed significantly to Botswana's long-term political stability. The people were not involved in its design and creation. In many respects, it was a colonial imposition or elitist at best.

This tension-between stability and participation, between elite design and popular ownership-lies at the heart of the constitutional review debate. Botswana's Constitution has served the nation well in many respects, providing a framework for peaceful governance and economic development. But the world has changed since 1966. Understandings of human rights have deepened. Expectations of democratic participation have risen. New challenges have emerged that the framers could not have anticipated.

Moreover, the legitimacy deficit at the Constitution's birth remains unaddressed. A Constitution that was negotiated without popular input, however well it has functioned, cannot command the same level of allegiance as one that the people have actively shaped and endorsed. As one chapter in this volume puts it, constitutional authority is weakened when people experience the Constitution as something "done to them," rather than "created by them."

The question, then, is not whether Botswana needs a constitutional review, but rather, what kind of review, undertaken through what kind of process and aimed at achieving what kind of transformation.

1.6 THE PATH FORWARD

This book is organised into two parts. Part One focuses on the foundations of the Constitution of Botswana. It begins by explaining the historical development of the Constitution, showing how Botswana's constitutional system came into being and how it has evolved. It then discusses why societies need government and introduces key ideas, such as republican government and constitutional government. These concepts help explain how power is obtained, exercised and limited in a democratic society.

Part One also explores how government can be organised in ways that prevent the abuse of power. It explains the importance of rules, institutions, and checks and balances in ensuring that those in authority act within the law. In addition, it highlights how the Constitution protects fundamental rights and freedoms, and why these protections are essential for human dignity, equality and justice.

Part Two of the book deals with Constitutional Review Process. It explains that reviewing a Constitution involves both process and content, and that these two aspects are equally important. The process refers to how a Constitution is reviewed, including who is involved and how decisions are made. The content refers to what changes are considered and why they may be necessary. Part Two also includes recommendations on how a Constitution can be reviewed in the best possible way, with the aim of ensuring legitimacy, public participation and respect for democratic values.

RECAP AND TRANSITION

Recap: This introductory chapter has traced the historical origins of Botswana's Constitution, from the Lancaster House Conference and Lobatse talks to its adoption at independence in 1966. It has explained the fundamental principles of constitutional supremacy, separation of powers, and the constitution as a living document belonging to the people. It has also highlighted the central tension that animates this book. While the Constitution has provided stability, its origins were elite-driven and lacked popular participation, creating a legitimacy deficit that a comprehensive review must address.

Transition: Having established the historical and conceptual foundations, the next chapter turns to a deeper philosophical question: If sovereignty belongs to the people, as democratic theory insists, why do free and sovereign individuals need government at all? And what does the answer to that question tell us about the nature of the constitutional compact between citizens and the state? Chapter Two explores these questions through the lens of popular sovereignty, social contract theory, and the political philosophy of John Locke, showing how these ideas illuminate Botswana's constitutional order and the stakes of constitutional review.

Chapter Two

POPULAR SOVEREIGNTY, GOVERNMENT AND SOCIAL CONTRACT

2.1 INTRODUCTION

Botswana is a constitutional democracy and a republic founded on the principles of the rule of law, popular sovereignty and representative government. Since independence in 1966, the country has maintained political stability, constitutionalism, and democratic governance, making it one of Africa's most enduring democracies. Central to Botswana's constitutional order is the idea that sovereign power originates from the people, commonly expressed through the phrase *"We the People"*

This chapter explores the philosophical and constitutional foundations of this idea and examines why a people, even as sovereign, require a government. Drawing particularly on the political philosophy of **John Locke**, this chapter analyses the concept of government formation, the meaning and function of the **social contract**, and the implications of that contract, especially the **right to rebellion**. The discussion is anchored in Botswana's status as a republic and constitutional democracy, linking theory to practical governance.

The questions explored in this chapter are not merely academic. They go to the heart of what it means to be a citizen in a constitutional democracy. If sovereignty belongs to the people, what does that require of those who govern? What obligations do citizens incur by accepting the protection of the state? And when, if ever, are citizens entitled to withdraw their consent and demand fundamental change? These questions resonate powerfully in the context of constitutional review, for they touch upon the very nature of the constitutional compact between the people and their government.

2.2 "WE THE PEOPLE" AS THE SOVEREIGN AUTHORITY

2.2.1 Meaning of Popular Sovereignty

The phrase *"We the People"* reflects the doctrine of **popular sovereignty**, which holds that all political power originates from the people rather than from a monarch, elite class or external authority. In a republic such as Botswana, sovereignty does not reside in the President, Parliament, or Judiciary but in the collective citizenry.

Popular sovereignty means:

- The people are the **ultimate source of authority**.
- Government exists **by consent**.
- Political power is **delegated**, not surrendered.

Botswana's Constitution embodies this principle by establishing institutions that derive legitimacy through elections and constitutional authority, rather than hereditary rule.

This understanding of sovereignty has profound implications for how we think about constitutional review. If power is delegated rather than surrendered, then the people who delegated that power retain the authority to redefine its scope, reallocate its functions, or withdraw it entirely and start anew. The Constitution is not a grant of power from the state to the people; it is a grant of power from the people to the state. This distinction, subtle but crucial, underpins the entire constitutional project.

2.2.2 Why Sovereignty Belongs to the People

Historically, sovereignty was often claimed by kings through divine right. Modern constitutional democracies reject this notion. Instead, sovereignty belongs to the people because:

- All individuals are born free and equal.
- No individual naturally has authority over another.
- Collective consent is the only legitimate basis for political power.

This principle aligns strongly with both African communal traditions and Western political philosophy, particularly Locke's natural rights theory.

In the African context, the idea that authority derives from the people resonates with traditional practices of consultation and consensus-building. The kgotla system, in which community members gather to discuss matters of common concern and reach decisions through dialogue, reflects a deep cultural commitment to participatory governance. While modern political systems have often sidelined these traditions, they remain part of Botswana's constitutional heritage and offer resources for thinking about how constitutional review might be conducted in a manner that is both democratic and culturally resonant.

2.3 WHY A SOVEREIGN PEOPLE NEED A GOVERNMENT

2.3.1 The Problem of Life Without Government

Although the people are sovereign, **absolute freedom without political organisation is impractical**. In the absence of government:

- Laws are unenforced.
- Rights are insecure.
- Disputes escalate into conflict.
- The strong dominate the weak.

Even if people possess natural rights, those rights require **institutional protection** to be meaningful.

The paradox of sovereignty is that freedom, to be secure, must be limited. Without government, individuals are free to do as they please, but their freedom is constantly threatened by others who are equally free. The strong can exploit the weak, disputes can escalate into violence and there is no impartial authority to resolve conflicts or enforce agreements. Government, properly constituted, does not diminish freedom; it creates the conditions under which freedom can be securely enjoyed.

2.3.2 Government as an Instrument of the People

In a constitutional democracy like Botswana:

- Government is not the master of the people.
- It is an **agent** of the people.
- Authority is exercised on behalf of the people.

Government exists to:

- Maintain law and order.
- Protect rights and freedoms.
- Promote peace and development.
- Provide public services.

Thus, while sovereignty remains with the people, governance is necessary to **organise collective life**.

This understanding of government as an agent rather than a master is central to constitutionalism. It implies that government officials are trustees of public power, not its owners. They hold authority on the condition that they exercise it for the public good and within the limits set by the Constitution. When they exceed those limits or betray that trust, they act without authority, and their actions are subject to challenge and correction.

2.4 JOHN LOCKE AND THE PHILOSOPHICAL FOUNDATIONS OF GOVERNMENT

2.4.1 Locke's State of Nature

John Locke argued that before government existed, humans lived in a **state of nature**, characterised by:

- Freedom
- Equality
- Natural rights to life, liberty and property

Unlike Thomas Hobbes, Locke did not believe the state of nature was chaotic, but he recognised serious weaknesses.

For Locke, the state of nature was not a war of all against all. It was a condition of freedom and equality, governed by the law of nature, which reason reveals and which teaches that no one ought to harm another in their life, health, liberty or possessions. Yet, despite this moral framework, the state of nature lacked certain essential features that only government could provide.

2.4.2 Problems in the State of Nature

Locke identified three major problems:

1. **No established law**: The law of nature, while binding in conscience, is not always clear to everyone and individuals may interpret it to suit their own interests.
2. **No impartial judge**: When disputes arise, there is no neutral authority to decide between conflicting claims.
3. **No effective enforcement**: Even when right is clear, there may be no power sufficient to enforce it against wrongdoers.

These deficiencies meant that, even though people had rights, those rights were constantly threatened.

Locke's analysis remains powerfully relevant. It explains why societies create governments: not to give them rights they did not previously possess, but to secure the rights they already have. Government is a remedy for the inconveniences of the state of nature. It provides what the state of nature lacks: settled laws, known by all; impartial judges to apply those laws; and effective enforcement to ensure compliance.

2.5 LOCKE'S INFLUENCE ON THE FORMATION OF GOVERNMENTS

2.5.1 Consent as the Basis of Legitimate Government

According to Locke:

- Governments are formed through **voluntary consent**.
- Political authority is legitimate only when people agree to it.
- Consent may be explicit (elections) or tacit (obeying laws).

Botswana's democratic elections are a clear expression of Lockean consent.

The requirement of consent has profound implications for constitutional legitimacy. A Constitution imposed by force, or negotiated without popular participation, lacks the consent that alone can make it binding in conscience. This is the fundamental critique of Botswana's 1966 Constitution; however, well-designed it may be, it was not consented to by the people it governs. Comprehensive constitutional review, conducted through an inclusive and participatory process, offers an opportunity to remedy this legitimacy deficit by securing the genuine consent of the governed.

2.5.2 Limited Government and Rule of Law

Locke argued that government power must be:

- Limited
- Bound by law
- Exercised for the public good

Botswana's Constitution reflects this by:

- Limiting executive power
- Establishing separation of powers
- Protecting fundamental rights

Limited government is the corollary of popular sovereignty. If the people are the ultimate source of authority, then those who exercise authority on their behalf can have no more power than the people have delegated. The Constitution specifies the scope and limits of that delegation, and any exercise of power beyond those limits is unauthorised and unlawful.

2.6 WHY PEOPLE NEED A GOVERNMENT ACCORDING TO LOCKE

Locke believed people form governments to:

- Secure natural rights
- Resolve disputes peacefully
- Protect property
- Ensure impartial justice

This rationale closely aligns with Botswana's post-independence constitutional goals of peace, unity and development.

The purposes for which government is formed also define the limits of governmental authority. Government may act only for the ends for which it was created-the security of rights, the peaceful resolution of disputes, the protection of property and the administration of impartial justice. When government acts for other ends, or when it uses means disproportionate to these ends, it exceeds its mandate and may be rightfully resisted.

2.7 THE SOCIAL CONTRACT EXPLAINED

2.7.1 Definition of a Social Contract

A **social contract** is an implicit or explicit agreement where:

- Individuals consent to give up some freedoms.
- In exchange for protection and order,
- Through an organised political authority

It is not a written contract, but a philosophical explanation of political obligation.

The social contract is not a historical event but a conceptual device for understanding the relationship between citizens and the state. It captures the idea that political authority rests on a kind of exchange: individuals agree to limit their freedom and submit to common rules, and, in return, the state agrees to provide security and protect rights. When either side fails to keep its part of the bargain, the contract is breached and the obligations it created may lapse.

2.7.2 The Social Contract in a Republic

In a republic like Botswana:

- Citizens accept laws and authority.
- Government agrees to govern justly.
- Power is exercised within constitutional limits.

This mutual agreement forms the moral and legal foundation of the state.

The social contract is not a one-time event but an ongoing relationship. It is renewed each time citizens obey the law, participate in elections, and engage in public life. It is also tested each time government exceeds its authority, violates rights or acts against the public interest. A Constitution that provides mechanisms for accountability-elections, judicial review, parliamentary oversight-creates channels through which the social contract can be renewed and repaired without resort to more drastic measures.

2.8 IMPLICATIONS OF THE SOCIAL CONTRACT

2.8.1 Rights and Duties of Citizens

Citizens are required to:

- Obey lawful authority
- Respect others' rights

- Participate in civic life

In return, they are entitled to:

- Protection of rights
- Equal treatment before the law
- Political participation

Citizenship is not passive. It carries obligations as well as rights. A constitutional democracy depends on citizens who are informed, engaged and willing to hold their government accountable. This is why constitutional literacy is so important: citizens cannot fulfil their role in the social contract if they do not understand the Constitution, their rights, and the institutions through which they can participate in governance.

2.8.2 Duties of Government

Government must:

- Act within constitutional limits
- Protect rights and freedoms
- Govern in the public interest

Failure to do so undermines the social contract.

The duties of government are the mirror image of the rights of citizens. Just as citizens owe obedience to lawful authority, government owes faithful execution of its trust. When government systematically fails in its duties, when it acts arbitrarily, violates rights or governs for private rather than public benefit, it breaks the social contract and forfeits its claim to obedience.

2.9 THE RIGHT TO REBELLION

2.9.1 Locke's Justification for Rebellion

Locke argued that rebellion is justified when:

- Government violates natural rights.
- Power is abused.
- Consent is withdrawn.

Rebellion is not anarchy; it is a defence of the original social contract.

Locke's argument for a right to rebellion is often misunderstood. He was not advocating for revolution at every grievance. Rather, he was making a conceptual point: if government is formed by consent for the protection of rights, then systematic violation of rights amounts to a dissolution of government. When government acts against the ends for which it was created, the people are entitled to defend themselves and to establish a new government that will serve those ends.

2.9.2 Rebellion and Constitutional Democracy

In modern constitutional systems:

- Legal mechanisms replace rebellion.
- Courts, elections and impeachment serve corrective roles.

Botswana's strong institutions reduce the need for violent rebellion by providing lawful avenues for accountability.

The genius of constitutional democracy is that it provides peaceful means for addressing the kinds of grievances that might otherwise lead to rebellion. Elections allow citizens to remove unsatisfactory rulers. Courts allow them to challenge unlawful actions. Parliament allows them to hold the Executive to account. These institutions do not eliminate the need for vigilance and civic engagement, but they channel political conflict into forms that can be resolved without violence.

2.10 BOTSWANA'S CONSTITUTIONAL ORDER AND THE SOCIAL CONTRACT

Botswana exemplifies a functioning social contract through:

- Regular, democratic elections
- Respect for judicial independence
- Protection of civil liberties

While challenges exist, the state's legitimacy rests on continued public consent and adherence to constitutional principles.

The social contract in Botswana is not merely theoretical. It is visible in the peaceful transfers of power that have marked the country's political history, in the willingness of citizens to accept court decisions, even when they disagree, and in the general respect for constitutional procedures. Yet, the social contract is not static. It must be renewed with each generation, and it must adapt to changing circumstances and expectations. Constitutional review is, in this sense, an opportunity to renew and deepen the social contract, to ensure that it continues to reflect the values and aspirations of the people it binds.

2.11 INCORPORATING THE STRUCTURE: TRADITIONAL INSTITUTIONS AND THE SOCIAL CONTRACT

Botswana's Constitution recognises customary law and traditional leadership as part of the social contract.

- **Ntlo ya Dikgosi**: Advises on issues affecting customary practices.
- **Customary courts**: Resolve disputes at community level.
- **Integration**: Customary law operates alongside statutory law, provided it does not conflict with constitutional principles.

The integration of traditional institutions into the constitutional order reflects a distinctive feature of Botswana's social contract. Unlike many post-colonial states that sought to displace customary authority with modern institutions, Botswana created a framework in which traditional leadership could coexist with democratic governance. The House of Chiefs (now Ntlo ya Dikgosi) provides advisory input, particularly on matters affecting customary law. Customary courts continue to resolve disputes at the community level, applying rules and procedures that are familiar and accessible to local populations.

Conflicts can arise between customary practices and constitutional rights, particularly in areas such as gender equality and non-discrimination. Resolving these conflicts requires careful attention to both constitutional principles and the legitimate claims of traditional communities.

The social contract in Botswana thus operates on multiple levels. At the national level, it is expressed through elections, legislation and judicial decisions. At the local level, it is expressed through customary institutions that enjoy deep roots in community life. A comprehensive constitutional review must attend to both levels, ensuring that the renewed social contract honours Botswana's traditions while also meeting contemporary standards of human rights and democratic governance.

2.12 CONCLUSION

The idea of *"We the People"* as sovereign lies at the heart of Botswana's constitutional democracy. While sovereignty belongs to the people, government is necessary to secure rights, maintain order, and promote collective well-being. John Locke's philosophy profoundly influenced this understanding by emphasising consent, limited government and the protection of natural rights.

The social contract provides both the moral justification for political authority and the conditions under which that authority may be challenged. In a republic like Botswana, the right to rebellion is largely transformed into constitutional and democratic remedies, ensuring stability while preserving popular sovereignty.

Ultimately, the strength of Botswana's democracy depends on the continuous honouring of the social contract between the people and their government.

The social contract is not a one-time agreement, but an ongoing relationship, sustained by institutions, practices and civic virtues. Constitutional review is an opportunity to renew that relationship, to ensure that it continues to reflect the values and aspirations of the people and to strengthen the institutions through which the people hold their government accountable.

RECAP AND TRANSITION

Recap: This chapter has explored the philosophical foundations of popular sovereignty and the social contract, drawing particularly on the political philosophy of John Locke. It has explained why sovereign people need government, how government is formed through consent and what obligations government and citizens owe each other under the social contract. It has also examined the right to rebellion and how modern constitutional democracies transform that right into peaceful legal mechanisms. Finally, it has considered how Botswana's integration of traditional institutions reflects a distinctive form of social contract operating at multiple levels.

Transition: Having established that Botswana is a constitutional democracy founded on popular sovereignty and the social contract, the next chapter turns to the specific form of government this social contract has produced. Chapter Three examines what it means for Botswana to be a "sovereign republic," exploring the principles of republicanism, representative government, and the electoral systems through which citizens delegate their sovereign authority to those who govern on their behalf.

Chapter Three

BOTSWANA IS A SOVEREIGN REPUBLIC

3.1 INTRODUCTION

Central to understanding Botswana's democracy are the ideas of republican government, representative government and electoral systems that structure political choice and governance. This chapter examines these concepts in depth, with specific emphasis on how they operate in Botswana's constitutional framework and political society.

The declaration that Botswana is a sovereign republic is not merely a formal title or an empty rhetorical flourish. It encapsulates fundamental choices about how political power is organised, where it originates and how it is to be exercised. To understand what it means to live in a republic is to understand the nature of citizenship, the basis of governmental authority, and the relationship between the people and those who govern on their behalf.

This chapter unfolds in three parts. First, it examines the concept of republican government, its core principles, and how these principles are embodied in Botswana's constitutional order. Second, it explores representative government as the mechanism through which republican ideals are translated into practice. Third, it analyses the electoral systems through which representation is structured, comparing Botswana's First Past-The-Post system with alternatives such as Proportional Representation, and considering the implications of each for democratic legitimacy and inclusive governance.

3.2 WHAT IS A REPUBLICAN GOVERNMENT?

3.2.1 Definition and Core Principles

A **republican government** is a political system in which:

- *Sovereignty resides with the people*, who elect representatives to govern on their behalf.
- The *head of state is not a hereditary monarch* but a person elected directly or indirectly.
- The *rule of law governs* the state, rather than arbitrary authority.

In republicanism, leaders are accountable to the people and must govern according to a written or entrenched Constitution that limits their power. The system emphasises **popular sovereignty, political equality and public virtue**, ensuring that public offices serve the common good rather than private interests.

The republican tradition has deep roots in political thought, extending back to ancient Rome and forward through the civic humanism of the Renaissance, the English Commonwealth period and the American and French revolutions. At its core lies a distinctive conception of freedom: to be free is not merely to be left alone by government, but to live under laws that one has a share in making, in a political community where no one is master over another. Freedom in a republic is freedom from domination, from subjection to the arbitrary will of another. This is achieved through institutions that disperse power, ensure accountability and give citizens a voice in public affairs.

3.2.2 Botswana's Constitutional Declaration of a Republic

The Constitution of Botswana explicitly declares the nation a republic.

The Constitution of Botswana declares, in ringing terms, in section 1, that **"Botswana is a sovereign Republic."**

This short but powerful declaration establishes Botswana's status as a sovereign democratic republic, meaning it derives its authority from the people of Botswana, and not from colonial or monarchical rule.

The placement of this declaration at the very beginning of the Constitution is significant. It announces, from the outset, that Botswana has rejected the forms of political organisation that characterised much of human history: rule by hereditary monarchs, rule by foreign powers, rule by those who claim divine right or military force. Instead, Botswana has chosen a form of government in which authority flows upward from the people, not downward from a ruler.

This choice was not inevitable. At independence, many newly sovereign states opted for different forms of government: some retained constitutional monarchies, with symbolic rulers and elected parliaments; others fell under military or one-party rule; still others adopted revolutionary ideologies that concentrated power in a single leader or movement. Botswana's commitment to republicanism, maintained consistently since 1966, reflects a deliberate and sustained choice for democratic self-government.

3.2.3 Practical Application in Botswana

Practically, Botswana's republicanism manifests in:

- **Periodic elections** are held every five years for the National Assembly and local councils.
- **Indirect election of the President,** whereby elected members of parliament choose the President from among themselves.
- **Civil liberties and fundamental rights** are guaranteed in Chapter II of the Constitution, emphasising equality regardless of race, political opinion, gender or origin.
- **An independent Judiciary**, which upholds the Constitution and protects individual rights.

These elements ensure that governance is based on law and consent, rather than tradition or coercion.

Periodic elections are the most visible expression of republican government. There are moments when the sovereign people exercise their authority directly, choosing who will represent them and govern on their behalf. The regularity of elections-every five years, with no interruptions since independence-creates a predictable cycle of accountability. Governments know they must face the people at regular intervals and this knowledge disciplines their conduct.

The indirect election of the President is a distinctive feature of Botswana's republicanism. Unlike many presidential systems, where the head of state is directly elected, Botswana's President emerges from and remains accountable to Parliament. This design choice reflects a preference for parliamentary supremacy and collective decision-making over the concentration of power in a single, popularly elected figure. It has contributed to political stability, but has also attracted criticism for insulating the President from direct popular accountability.

The guarantee of civil liberties and fundamental rights in Chapter II of the Constitution reflects the republican commitment to political equality. These rights ensure that all citizens, regardless of their social position or political views, can participate in public life and challenge governmental action. They are not merely aspirational; they are enforceable through the courts, which have shown themselves willing to give them practical effect.

An independent Judiciary is essential to republicanism because it ensures that the limits on governmental power are real, rather than merely rhetorical. Courts that can strike down unconstitutional laws and invalidate unlawful executive action serve as guardians of the constitutional order. They protect the people's sovereign authority against encroachment by those who exercise delegated power.

3.3 ADVANTAGES OF A REPUBLICAN GOVERNMENT

3.3.1 Accountability and Representation

Republican governments emphasise the accountability of leaders to the people. Elected officials must justify their decisions to constituents and face re-election or replacement if they fail to serve the public interest.

Accountability operates through multiple channels. Elections are the primary mechanism, allowing citizens to pass judgement on their representatives at regular intervals. But accountability also operates between elections, through parliamentary oversight, media scrutiny, civil society advocacy, and judicial review. A robust republican system ensures that officials are answerable not only at the ballot box, but throughout their terms of office.

3.3.2 Protection of Rights

A republican constitution, like Botswana's, entrenches fundamental rights and freedoms that protect individuals against the arbitrary actions of the state. This fosters political stability and social trust.

The entrenchment of rights means that they cannot be altered by ordinary legislation or executive action. They stand above day-to-day politics, representing fundamental commitments that bind all branches of government. This protects individuals and minorities from the tyranny of the majority, ensuring that even popular governments respect basic freedoms.

3.3.3 Legitimacy and Popular Sovereignty

Leaders derive their legitimacy from the people's mandate. Botswana's regular elections and peaceful transfers of power, including the 2024 shift of power, demonstrate the legitimacy of its republican framework.

The peaceful transfer of power from one party to another, when it occurs, is a powerful testament to the strength of republican institutions. It shows that those who lose power accept the legitimacy of their loss and that those who gain power respect the limits of their mandate. This self-restraint, exercised by both winners and losers, is the hallmark of a mature republican culture.

3.3.4 Rule of Law

Republicanism places law above any individual. Botswana's judiciary can strike down unlawful acts, reinforcing checks and balances.

The rule of law means that no one is above the law-not the President, not the Parliament, not the military, not the police. All must act within the bounds set by law and all are subject to the jurisdiction of the courts. This principle is foundational to republicanism because it prevents the emergence of arbitrary power.

3.4 DISADVANTAGES OF A REPUBLICAN GOVERNMENT

3.4.1 Risk of Majoritarian Dominance

Republican systems that rely on simple majorities can marginalise minority voices if electoral systems do not ensure proportional representation. Botswana's dominance by a single party for decades reflects this challenge.

Majoritarian dominance is not necessarily a sign of failure. It may reflect genuine popular support for a particular party or programme. But it carries risks. When one party dominates for extended periods, the distinction between party and state can blur. Opposition voices may be marginalised, dissent may be discouraged and the institutions of accountability may weaken. Constitutional design must anticipate these risks and build in safeguards that protect minority interests, even when one party holds a commanding majority.

3.4.2 Electoral Instability

Because republican governments depend on periodic elections, they can be vulnerable to political fragmentation or instability if institutions are weak or electoral integrity is compromised.

Elections are moments of uncertainty. They can produce unexpected outcomes, fragmented parliaments, or contested results. Strong institutions-independent electoral commissions, impartial courts, professional civil services-are needed to manage this uncertainty and ensure that elections strengthen rather than destabilise the political order.

3.4.3 Potential for Executive Overreach

In some democracies, republican institutions may concentrate power in the executive, diminishing legislative oversight. Critics argue that Botswana's system sometimes reflects strong executive dominance.

Executive dominance is a recurring concern in republican thought. The Executive, by its nature, has advantages in information, initiative and resources. It can act quickly and decisively, while legislatures deliberate slowly and publicly. Over time, these advantages can lead to a shift in the balance of power, with the Executive increasingly setting the agenda and the legislature merely ratifying its decisions. Constitutional design must attend to this risk, ensuring that legislatures have the capacity and authority to hold executives accountable.

3.5 WHAT IS REPRESENTATIVE GOVERNMENT?

3.5.1 Definition

Representative government is a system where citizens elect individuals to represent their interests in legislative and executive bodies. It contrasts with direct democracy, where citizens vote on policy issues themselves rather than for representatives.

Representative government is a practical necessity in modern states. Direct democracy, in which citizens assemble to make decisions collectively, is possible only in small communities. In large, complex societies, with millions of citizens spread over vast territories, representation is the only feasible form of democratic governance. Citizens choose representatives who deliberate on their behalf, bringing diverse perspectives and expertise to bear on the challenges of governance.

3.5.2 Features of Representative Government

- Regular, competitive elections
- Representatives act on behalf of constituents to make laws and policies
- A framework of institutions (legislature, executive, judiciary) balances power
- Political parties organise and aggregate interests

Regular, competitive elections ensure that representatives remain accountable to those they represent. If citizens are dissatisfied with their representative's performance, they can choose someone else at the next election. This creates incentives for responsiveness and good performance.

Representatives act on behalf of constituents, but they are not mere delegates bound by instructions. They exercise judgement, weighing competing interests and considering the common good. This trustee conception of representation, rooted in the republican tradition, recognises that representatives must sometimes make unpopular decisions that serve long-term interests.

A framework of institutions balances power and prevents any single actor from dominating. The legislature makes laws, the Executive implements them, and the Judiciary interprets them and ensures they conform to constitutional requirements. This separation of powers, discussed in earlier chapters, is essential to representative government.

Political parties organise and aggregate interests. They simplify electoral choice, provide voters with information about candidates and programmes and structure legislative decision-making. While parties are often criticised for pursuing partisan advantage, they are indispensable to modern representative democracy.

3.5.3 Botswana's Application of Representative Government

In Botswana, representative democracy operates primarily through:

- **Universal adult suffrage** for voters 18 years and above.
- **National Assembly elections**, where MPs represent single-member constituencies under a first-past-the-post system.
- **The indirect election of the President** by Parliament reflects the representative mandate.
- A blend of traditional and modern governance (e.g., Kgotla meetings and the advisory House of Chiefs) that integrates popular participation with representative structures.

Representative government in Botswana balances direct community participation at local levels with national representative institutions.

Universal adult suffrage ensures that all citizens, regardless of wealth, education, or social status, have an equal voice in choosing their representatives. This is fundamental to political equality and republican government.

National Assembly elections, conducted every five years, determine the composition of Parliament and, indirectly, the identity of the President. Members of Parliament represent single-member constituencies, creating a direct link between each community and its representative. This constituency link is a strength of Botswana's system, fostering accountability and responsiveness.

The indirect election of the President by Parliament reflects a design choice that prioritises parliamentary supremacy and collective decision-making. While it insulates the President from direct popular election, it also ensures that the President emerges from and remains accountable to the representative body.

The blend of traditional and modern governance is distinctive. Kgotla meetings, in which community members gather to discuss matters of common concern, provide a forum for direct participation at the local level. The House of Chiefs (Ntlo ya Dikgosi) gives traditional leaders an advisory role in national affairs, particularly on matters affecting customary law and practice. This integration of traditional institutions into a modern representative framework reflects Botswana's effort to honour its heritage while embracing democratic governance.

3.6 WHICH ELECTORAL SYSTEM DOES BOTSWANA FOLLOW?

Botswana uses the **First-Past-The-Post (FPTP)** electoral system for National Assembly and local government elections. Under this system:

- The country is divided into **single-member constituencies**.
- Voters cast a ballot for a candidate.
- The candidate with the **most votes** wins the seat.

There is **no direct presidential election**; the President is chosen by members of the National Assembly.

The First-Past-The-Post system is one of the oldest and simplest electoral systems. It is used in many countries with British constitutional heritage, including the United Kingdom, Canada, India and Botswana. Its simplicity is a virtue: voters understand it, results are clear, and governments are usually formed quickly without complex coalition negotiations.

However, FPTP also has well-documented limitations. It can produce disproportionate outcomes, where a party's share of seats does not match its share of votes. It can marginalise smaller parties and minority voices. It can leave large segments of the electorate without effective representation. These limitations have prompted debates about electoral reform in many FPTP countries, including Botswana.

3.7 ADVANTAGES AND DISADVANTAGES OF BOTSWANA'S ELECTORAL SYSTEM

3.7.1 Advantages of FPTP

3.7.1.1 Simplicity

The system is easy to understand and administer, requiring no complex calculations.

Simplicity matters. Electoral systems that are difficult to understand can alienate voters and create opportunities for manipulation. FPTP's straightforward mechanism-vote for one candidate, the candidate with the most votes wins-is accessible to all voters, regardless of education or literacy.

3.7.1.2 Strong Constituency Link

Voters know their individual MP, facilitating accountability and local responsiveness.

Each constituency has a single, identifiable representative. Voters know who to contact with concerns, who to praise for good performance, and who to blame for neglect. This constituency link creates incentives for MPs to attend to local needs and maintain visibility in their communities.

3.7.1.3 Political Stability

FPTP often produces stable majorities, enabling decisive governance without fragile coalition politics.

Stability is a significant advantage. Governments formed under FPTP typically have clear majorities, allowing them to implement their programmes without constant negotiation with coalition partners. This can lead to decisive action and policy continuity.

3.7.2 Disadvantages of FPTP

3.7.2.1 Disproportionality

FPTP often leads to mismatches between votes won and seats allocated. A party with a sizeable vote share may receive few seats, while another with fewer votes may dominate in seats.

Disproportionality is the most persistent criticism of FPTP. It means that the composition of Parliament may not reflect the actual distribution of voter preferences. This can undermine the perceived legitimacy of electoral outcomes and leave significant segments of the electorate feeling unrepresented.

3.7.2.2 Marginalisation of Minor Parties

Smaller parties and independent voices can struggle to secure representation, weakening diversity in Parliament.

FPTP tends to favour larger, established parties and disadvantage smaller or newer ones. This can limit the range of perspectives in Parliament and reduce competition. Over time, it may contribute to voter apathy, as supporters of smaller parties may feel their votes are wasted.

3.7.2.3 Debate Over Fairness

While stable, FPTP is criticised for not fully reflecting voter preferences or creating truly representative outcomes.

Fairness is a contested concept in electoral system design. FPTP proponents argue that it is fair because it treats all constituencies equally and produces clear winners. Critics argue that true fairness requires proportionality, that a party's seat share should roughly match its vote share. This debate has no settled resolution; it reflects deeper disagreements about what representation should mean.

3.8 WHAT IS PROPORTIONAL REPRESENTATION (PR)?

3.8.1 Definition

Proportional representation (PR) is an electoral system in which:

- Seats in a legislature are allocated **in proportion** to the number of votes each party receives.
- Rather than single-member districts, voters may choose parties on a list, and seats are distributed according to vote share.

This system seeks a closer match between electoral support and legislative representation.

PR systems come in many varieties. Some use party lists, with voters choosing among parties, and seats allocated according to each party's share of the vote. Others use mixed systems, combining single-member districts with proportional top-ups. Still others use single transferable votes, allowing voters to rank candidates within and across parties. Despite this diversity, all PR systems share the core principle of proportionality: the legislature should reflect, as closely as possible, the distribution of voter preferences.

3.9 ADVANTAGES AND DISADVANTAGES OF PROPORTIONAL REPRESENTATION

3.9.1 Advantages of PR

3.9.1.1 Fair Representation

PR ensures that political parties' share of seats reflects their popular vote, promoting inclusiveness and legitimacy.

Fair representation is the primary argument for PR. When seats match votes, every vote counts. Voters can support their preferred party without worrying about wasting their vote, and the resulting legislature reflects the diversity of public opinion.

3.9.1.2 Enhanced Minor Party Participation

Smaller parties have better chances of entering Parliament, enriching political debate.

PR systems typically produce more diverse legislatures, with multiple parties representing a range of perspectives. This can enrich debate, encourage compromise and ensure that minority voices are heard.

3.9.1.3 Reduced Wasted Votes

Most votes contribute to seat allocation, encouraging voter engagement.

Under FPTP, votes for losing candidates do not affect the composition of Parliament. Under PR, almost all votes contribute to seat allocation. This can increase voter turnout and engagement, as citizens see a clearer connection between their votes and the outcome.

3.9.2 Disadvantages of PR

3.9.2.1 Coalition Politics

PR often leads to coalition governments that may be less stable or decisive than single-party administrations.

Coalition governments require negotiation and compromise. This can slow decision-making and produce policies that reflect bargains among parties, rather than coherent programmes. In some cases, coalitions can be fragile, collapsing over disagreements and forcing new elections.

3.9.2.2 Weaker Constituency Link

Because representatives are chosen from party lists, the direct link between constituents and specific legislators can weaken.

In list-based PR systems, representatives are accountable to their parties rather than to geographic constituencies. This can weaken the connection between citizens and their representatives, reducing local accountability and responsiveness.

3.9.2.3 Complexity

PR systems can be more complex to administer and may confuse voters unfamiliar with party lists.

Some PR systems, particularly those with complex formulas or multi-tier allocations, can be difficult for voters to understand. This complexity can undermine transparency and trust.

3.10 INCORPORATING THE STRUCTURE: CHECKS AND BALANCES IN BOTSWANA'S REPUBLIC

The Constitution establishes mechanisms to prevent abuse of power:

- **Parliamentary oversight**: Ministers are accountable to the National Assembly.
- **Judicial review**: Courts can invalidate unconstitutional actions.
- **Independent institutions**: Bodies such as the Ombudsman provide additional safeguards.

These mechanisms give practical effect to republican principles. Parliamentary oversight ensures that the executive, which holds significant power, is regularly called to account. Ministers must answer questions, defend their decisions and justify their use of public resources. This scrutiny, conducted in public, reinforces the republican principle that power is delegated, not owned.

Judicial review empowers courts to strike down actions that violate the Constitution. This is a powerful check on both legislative and executive power. It ensures that even when political actors have majority support, they cannot override constitutional limits. The Ombudsman's investigations into administrative misconduct demonstrate how checks and balances protect citizens from abuse.

Independent institutions like the Ombudsman, the Auditor General and the Independent Electoral Commission serve as guardians of integrity. They operate outside the normal chain of command. Their independence allows them to investigate wrongdoing without fear or favour, strengthening accountability and public trust.

The amendment process also reflects republican principles. The Constitution provides mechanisms for amendment to ensure adaptability.

- **Parliamentary procedure**: Amendments require approval by the National Assembly.
- **Safeguards**: Fundamental rights provisions are more difficult to amend, protecting core values.

The ability to amend the Constitution allows it to adapt to changing circumstances. But amendment is not easy; it requires broad consensus and careful deliberation. This balance between flexibility and stability is characteristic of republican constitutionalism. The entrenchment of certain provisions, making them harder to amend, reflects a judgement that some values are so fundamental that they should not be subject to ordinary political contestation.

3.11 CONCLUSION

Botswana's constitutional democracy is grounded in republicanism and representative government. Its written Constitution enshrines the nation's status as a republic and guarantees fundamental rights. Botswana's electoral system: First-Past-The-Post has helped sustain political stability and accountability, but also presents challenges concerning proportional representation and inclusiveness. Understanding these concepts clarifies both the strengths and areas for potential reform in Botswana's democratic practice.

The republican tradition offers enduring insights for constitutional design. It teaches that freedom requires more than the absence of interference;

it requires institutions that prevent domination and ensure that citizens have a voice in their governance. It teaches that power must be dispersed and checked, that officials must be accountable and that law must bind all equally. These insights are as relevant today as when they were first articulated.

Botswana's Republic has endured for more than half a century. It has provided stability, protected rights, and enabled development. But endurance does not mean perfection. The challenges identified in this chapter-majoritarian dominance, executive overreach, electoral disproportionality-are real and warrant attention. Constitutional review offers an opportunity to address them, to strengthen republican institutions and to deepen democratic practice.

RECAP AND TRANSITION

Recap: This chapter has explored the meaning of republican government and its embodiment in Botswana's constitutional order. It has defined republicanism, examined its advantages and disadvantages, and analysed how Botswana's Constitution gives effect to republican principles through periodic elections, an indirectly elected President, entrenched rights, and an independent judiciary. It has also examined representative government and electoral systems, comparing Botswana's First-Past-The-Post system with Proportional Representation and considering the implications of each for democratic legitimacy and inclusive governance. Finally, it has incorporated structural elements from Botswana's Constitution-checks and balances, independent institutions, amendment procedures-to show how republican principles are given practical effect.

Transition: Having established that Botswana is a sovereign republic with representative institutions and a particular electoral system, the next chapter turns to the framework that makes all of this possible: constitutional democracy itself. Chapter Four examines what it means for a government to be both constitutional and democratic, exploring concepts such as constitutionalism, the rule of law, separation of powers and good governance. It explains how these ideas work together to prevent abuse of power and protect the rights and freedoms of citizens.

Chapter Four

CONSTITUTIONAL DEMOCRACY

4.1 INTRODUCTION

Constitutional democracy lies at the heart of Botswana's political and legal order. It ensures that government authority is exercised according to agreed constitutional rules, subject to accountability, and for the benefit of the people.

This chapter explains the concept of constitutional democracy and its key components. It explores constitutional government, constitutionalism, the rule of law, good governance, separation of powers, checks and balances, and the protection of human rights, with reference to Botswana. It also discusses why political thinkers feared abuse of power and how constitutional design seeks to prevent it.

The term "constitutional democracy" joins two ideas that are sometimes in tension. Democracy speaks of popular rule, of government by the people, of majority decision-making. Constitutionalism speaks of limits on government, of constraints on what majorities can do, of fundamental law that stands above ordinary politics. A constitutional democracy is an attempt to reconcile these ideas: to create a system in which the people govern, but within bounds that protect fundamental rights and prevent tyranny.

This chapter explores how Botswana's constitutional order attempts this reconciliation. It examines the mechanisms through which power is both granted and limited, the institutions through which the people govern and hold their governors accountable, and the principles that distinguish constitutional democracy from mere majoritarianism.

4.2 WHAT IS A CONSTITUTIONAL GOVERNMENT

A **constitutional government** is a system of government in which the powers of the state are defined, limited and regulated by a constitution. Government authority does not arise from the will of rulers alone, but from the supreme law of the land.

In a constitutional government:

- Government officials exercise power **within legal limits**.
- The Constitution is **supreme over all persons and institutions**.
- Citizens have enforceable rights against the state.
- Independent courts ensure compliance with the Constitution.

In Botswana, the Constitution binds the Executive, Legislature, Judiciary, and all public authorities. Any law or action inconsistent with the Constitution may be declared invalid by the courts.

Constitutional government stands in contrast to arbitrary government, where rulers exercise power according to their will rather than according to law. In an arbitrary government, there are no effective limits on what those in power can do. They may make laws, but they do not bind them. They may create courts, but those courts cannot hold them accountable. They may proclaim rights, but those rights cannot be enforced against them.

Constitutional government rejects this model. It insists that even those who hold the highest offices are subject to law. The President must obey the Constitution. Parliament must legislate within its powers. The police must respect the rights of citizens. And when any of these actors overstep, the courts have the authority to intervene. This is what it means to have a government of laws, not of men.

4.3 WHAT IS A CONSTITUTION?

A **constitution** is a foundational legal document that sets out:

- The structure of government.
- The distribution of powers.

- The relationship between the state and the individual.
- Fundamental rights and freedoms
- Procedures for governance and constitutional amendment.

The Constitution of Botswana is a **written constitution** and is the **supreme law.**

A Constitution performs three major functions:

1. **Empowering government** – creating institutions and granting authority
2. **Limiting power** – preventing abuse and arbitrariness
3. **Protecting rights** – safeguarding individual freedoms

A Constitution is both a grant of power and a limitation on power. It creates institutions—a Legislature, an Executive, a Judiciary-and gives them authority to act. But it also sets boundaries on that authority, specifying what these institutions may and may not do. And it protects the rights of individuals against encroachment by the state.

This dual character is essential. Without empowerment, government cannot function. Without limitation, government becomes tyrannical. A Constitution that empowers without limiting invites abuse. A Constitution that limits without empowering invites chaos. The art of constitutional design lies in striking the right balance: creating institutions strong enough to govern effectively but constrained enough to respect rights and maintain accountability.

4.4 WHAT IS CONSTITUTIONALISM?

Constitutionalism is the belief and practice that government power must be limited by law and exercised in accordance with constitutional principles. It goes beyond the mere existence of a Constitution.

Key elements of constitutionalism include:

- Limited government
- Respect for fundamental rights

- Separation of powers
- Judicial review
- Accountability and transparency

A country may have a Constitution without constitutionalism if leaders ignore constitutional limits. Botswana's adherence to constitutionalism is reflected in respect for court decisions, regular elections and institutional stability.

The distinction between having a Constitution and practising constitutionalism is crucial. Many countries have constitutions on paper, but not in practice. Their leaders ignore constitutional limits when convenient. Their courts cannot enforce constitutional provisions against powerful interests. Their citizens' rights exist in theory, but not in reality.

Constitutionalism requires more than a document. It requires a culture of respect for constitutional limits, an independent Judiciary with the courage to enforce those limits, a civil society that defends constitutional values, and a citizenry that understands and claims its rights. It requires, in short, that the Constitution be lived as well as written.

Botswana's record on constitutionalism is generally strong. Courts have issued decisions against the government, and those decisions have been respected. Elections have been held regularly, and their results accepted. Independent institutions have operated without interference. But constitutionalism is never permanently secured. It requires constant vigilance and renewal.

4.5 WHAT IS THE RULE OF LAW?

The **rule of law** means that:

- Everyone is subject to the law, including government officials.
- Laws are clear, public and applied equally.
- Independent courts enforce legal rights.
- Arbitrary exercise of power is prohibited.

In Botswana, the rule of law is upheld through:

- An independent Judiciary
- Due process and fair trial rights
- Judicial review of executive and legislative actions

The rule of law ensures that power is exercised through legal authority, not personal discretion.

The rule of law is a complex idea with multiple dimensions. At its core, it means that law, not will, governs. Decisions are made according to pre-announced rules, not according to the whim of officials. Those rules apply equally to all, not differently to favourites and disfavours. And they are enforced by courts that are independent of those who make and execute the laws.

The rule of law has both formal and substantive aspects. Formally, it requires that laws be clear, public, stable and applied generally. Substantively, it requires that laws respect fundamental rights and human dignity. A system that clearly and consistently applies oppressive laws would satisfy the formal rule of law but violate its substantive dimension. Modern understandings of the rule of law encompass both aspects: law must be both properly enacted and fundamentally just.

Botswana's courts have played a significant role in upholding the rule of law. In cases ranging from criminal procedure to constitutional rights, they have insisted that the government act according to law and have provided remedies when it fails to do so. This judicial vigilance is essential to maintaining the rule of law over time.

4.6 WHAT IS GOOD GOVERNANCE?

Good governance refers to the way public authority is exercised for the common good. It emphasises ethical leadership and effective administration.

Principles of good governance include:

- Accountability
- Transparency
- Participation
- Responsiveness
- Efficiency and effectiveness
- Respect for the rule of law

Botswana's governance framework promotes good governance through democratic elections, parliamentary oversight and independent institutions, such as the courts and the Auditor General.

Good governance is about how power is exercised, not just how it is structured. It concerns the quality of decision-making, the integrity of officials, the responsiveness of institutions, and the extent to which citizens can participate in and influence public affairs.

Accountability means that officials must answer for their actions. They must explain their decisions, justify their use of resources, and accept consequences when they fail. Accountability operates through multiple channels: elections, parliamentary oversight, judicial review, media scrutiny and civil society advocacy.

Transparency means that the government operates openly. Citizens can see what their government is doing, understand how decisions are made and access information about public affairs. Transparency enables accountability by providing the information citizens need to judge their government's performance.

Participation means that citizens have opportunities to influence decisions that affect them. This includes voting in elections, but also engaging in public consultations, joining civil society organisations, and communicating with elected representatives. Participation deepens democracy by ensuring that diverse perspectives inform public policy.

Efficiency and effectiveness mean that the government achieves its objectives without wasting resources. Good governance is not just about process; it is about results. Institutions must be capable of delivering the services and protections citizens expect.

4.7 PREVENTING ABUSE OF POWER THROUGH GOVERNMENT STRUCTURE

Abuse of power occurs when authority is exercised arbitrarily, unfairly, or for personal gain. Constitutional democracies prevent abuse by structuring government power carefully.

Key mechanisms include:

- Separation of powers
- Checks and balances
- Regular elections
- Independent judiciary
- Clear legal limits on authority

By dispersing power among different institutions, no single authority dominates the system.

The problem of power is central to constitutional design. Power is necessary: without it, government cannot protect rights, provide services or maintain order. But power is also dangerous: those who hold it are tempted to abuse it, to use it for private gain rather than public good, to extend it beyond its proper bounds.

Constitutional democracy addresses this problem by dispersing power. Instead of concentrating authority in a single person or institution, it distributes it among multiple actors, each with its own sphere of responsibility and each capable of checking the others. This dispersion makes abuse more difficult because any actor seeking to overreach must overcome the resistance of others.

4.8 FEAR OF ABUSE OF POWER: VIEWS OF POLITICAL THINKERS

Leading political thinkers warned that unchecked power inevitably leads to tyranny.

Alexander Hamilton

Hamilton cautioned against concentrating all power in one body and suggested that giving all power to the many is as dangerous as giving it to the few.

This highlights the need for institutional restraints, even in democracies.

Benjamin Franklin

Franklin observed that:

"There are two passions which have a powerful influence on the affairs of men: these are ambition and avarice (greed); love of power and the love of money."

This insight explains why constitutional safeguards are necessary to restrain human self-interest.

George Mason

George Mason famously warned:

"From the nature of man, we may be sure that those who have power in their hands will always, when they can, increase it."

These views influenced constitutional design, emphasising limited government and accountability.

The insights of these thinkers remain relevant. Human nature does not change when people enter government. The same ambitions, the same self-interest, the same desire for power and wealth that operate in private life operate in public life as well. Constitutional design must take this reality seriously. It must create institutions that channel ambition toward public good and that make abuse difficult, even for those inclined toward it.

This is not cynicism; it is realism. Institutions that assume officials will always act virtuously are doomed to fail. Institutions that anticipate the possibility of abuse and build in safeguards against it are more likely to endure. The challenge is to create systems that work with human nature as it is, not as we might wish it to be.

4.9 SEPARATION OF POWERS AND HOW IT WORKS

The separation of powers divides government authority among three branches:

- **Legislature** – makes laws.
- **Executive** – implements laws
- **Judiciary** – interprets laws

In Botswana:

- Parliament enacts legislation.
- The Executive (President and Cabinet) governs.
- The Judiciary adjudicates disputes and enforces constitutional limits.

Each branch operates independently but cooperatively, preventing concentration of power.

The separation of powers serves multiple functions. It promotes efficiency by allowing each branch to specialise in its core functions. It protects liberty by ensuring that no single actor can make, enforce, and interpret laws all by itself. It creates accountability by giving each branch incentives to monitor the others.

The separation is not absolute. In practice, branches interact and overlap. The Executive proposes legislation and implements laws passed by the Legislature. The Legislature oversees the executive and appropriates funds for its operations. The Judiciary interprets laws made by the Legislature and applied by the Executive, and its interpretations can prompt legislative revision. These interactions are features, not bugs, of constitutional design. They create the checks and balances that prevent any branch from dominating.

4.10 CHECKS AND BALANCES

Checks and balances allow each branch to restrain the others.

Examples in Botswana include:

- Parliament scrutinising executive actions
- Courts reviewing the constitutionality of laws
- The Executive assents to, or vetoes, legislation

This system ensures accountability and prevents dominance by any one branch.

Checks and balances give each branch weapons it can use to defend its prerogatives and resist encroachment. Parliament can refuse to pass Executive proposals, can reject Executive appointments, can demand information and explanations from ministers. Courts can strike down laws that exceed legislative authority or violate constitutional rights. The Executive can veto legislation it considers unwise or unconstitutional.

These checks create a dynamic equilibrium. No branch can simply impose its will on the others; each must persuade, negotiate and compromise. This makes government slower and more cumbersome, but it also makes it more deliberative and less prone to arbitrary action. The friction created by checks and balances is a feature, not a bug: it slows down government enough to allow reflection and to mobilise opposition to ill-considered measures.

4.11 ROLE OF PARLIAMENT

Parliament plays a central role in constitutional democracy:

Law-Making

Parliament debates, amends and enacts laws.

Representation

Members of Parliament represent citizens' interests and concerns.

Oversight and Accountability

Parliament:

- Questions ministers
- Reviews government spending
- Holds the Executive accountable through committees and debates

This watchdog function strengthens democratic governance. The Constitution instructs Parliament to exercise its power of law-making to: "make laws for the peace, order and good government of Botswana".

Parliament is the institution through which the people's representatives deliberate on matters of public concern. It is where laws are made, budgets are approved and governments are held to account. A strong Parliament is essential to constitutional democracy.

The law-making function is Parliament's most visible role. Bills are introduced, debated, amended and ultimately passed or rejected. This process allows for public input, expert testimony and deliberation among competing views. It ensures that the Executive does not simply decree laws but is subject to scrutiny by representatives of the people.

The representation function connects citizens to their government. Members of Parliament bring the concerns of their constituents to the national stage. They advocate for local interests, raise issues affecting their communities and provide a channel through which citizens can influence national policy.

The oversight function holds the executive accountable. Through parliamentary questions, committee hearings, and debates, Parliament scrutinises executive actions and demands explanations. It reviews government spending to ensure that public funds are used properly. It can summon ministers to answer for their departments' performance. This oversight is essential to preventing abuse of power and maintaining public trust.

4.12 BILL OF RIGHTS IN BOTSWANA

The **Bill of Rights** in Chapter II of the Constitution of Botswana protects fundamental freedoms, including:

- Right to life
- Protection from inhuman treatment
- Freedom of expression
- Freedom of assembly and association
- Right to a fair trial
- Protection of property

These rights are enforceable through the courts.

The Bill of Rights is the Constitution's most direct protection of individual liberty. It sets out rights that government must respect and that individuals can enforce against government. These rights are not merely aspirational; they are legally binding and judicially enforceable.

The rights protected in Botswana's Constitution reflect the influence of international human rights instruments and comparative constitutional practice. They include both traditional civil liberties: freedom of expression, assembly, association; and protections for specific interests: life, property, fair trial. Together, they create a framework within which government must operate and against which its actions can be measured.

The enforceability of these rights through the courts is crucial. Rights that cannot be enforced are not rights in any meaningful sense; they are merely declarations of good intentions. Botswana's courts have shown themselves willing to enforce constitutional rights, issuing decisions that have protected individuals against governmental overreach and given practical effect to constitutional guarantees.

4.13 LIMITATIONS OF THE BILL OF RIGHTS IN BOTSWANA

The Bill of Rights mainly entrenches **civil and political rights**. It does not expressly protect:

- Socio-economic rights (health, housing, education)
- Environmental rights
- Explicit gender equality clauses

Some rights are also subject to limitations, "reasonably justifiable in a democratic society," which may restrict their scope.

The limitations of Botswana's Bill of Rights reflect its origins in the 1960s, when constitutional rights were typically understood as protections against state interference rather than positive entitlements to state provision. The rights protected are primarily negative: rights to be free from certain kinds of governmental action, rather than rights to receive certain benefits from government.

This approach leaves important interests unprotected. Access to healthcare, education, housing, and other necessities is not constitutionally guaranteed, even though they are essential to human flourishing and dignity. Citizens cannot go to court to demand that the government provide these services, however inadequate the provision may be.

Environmental rights are also absent. Given the importance of environmental protection to sustainable development and human well-being, this omission is increasingly significant. Many modern constitutions include environmental rights or principles, recognising that environmental degradation threatens other rights and interests.

The limitation clauses in the Bill of Rights allow rights to be restricted for specified purposes, provided the restrictions are "reasonably justifiable in a democratic society." This formulation gives courts significant discretion to balance rights against competing public interests. While flexibility is valuable, it also creates uncertainty about the scope of protection.

4.14 ROOM FOR IMPROVEMENT IN THE BILL OF RIGHTS

Possible improvements include:

- Inclusion of socio-economic rights
- Stronger equality and non-discrimination provisions
- Explicit protection of vulnerable groups
- Greater clarity on limitation clauses

Such reforms would strengthen constitutional protection.

The limitations identified in the previous section are not inevitable. They can be addressed through constitutional reform, as many countries have done in recent decades. Modern Constitutions increasingly include socio-economic rights, recognising that freedom is hollow without the material conditions to enjoy it. They include detailed equality provisions, addressing discrimination on multiple grounds and requiring affirmative measures to address historical disadvantage. They explicitly protect vulnerable groups - children, persons with disabilities, indigenous communities-recognising that general rights provisions may not adequately address their specific situations.

Such reforms would not be without challenges. Socio-economic rights raise difficult questions about justiciability and enforcement. Courts cannot easily determine how much government should spend on healthcare or education, or how to prioritise among competing needs. But these challenges are not insurmountable. Courts in South Africa, India, and other countries have developed sophisticated approaches to enforcing socio-economic rights, focusing on reasonableness, progressive realisation and non-retrogression rather than imposing fixed obligations.

4.15 ADVANTAGES OF AN EXPANSIVE BILL OF RIGHTS

An expansive Bill of Rights:

- Enhances human dignity
- Promotes social justice
- Strengthens accountability
- Aligns domestic law with international human rights standards
- Empowers courts to protect marginalised groups

It deepens democracy by ensuring that freedom is both political and social.

An expansive Bill of Rights recognises that human dignity requires more than freedom from state interference. It requires access to the material conditions necessary for a decent life. It requires protection against private, as well as public, power. It requires attention to the situations of groups that have historically been disadvantaged.

By including socio-economic rights, a constitution acknowledges that poverty and deprivation are as threatening to human dignity as arbitrary arrest or censorship. By including detailed equality provisions, it acknowledges that formal legal equality is insufficient to address deep-seated social hierarchies. By protecting vulnerable groups explicitly, it ensures that constitutional rights reach those who need them most.

An expansive Bill of Rights also strengthens accountability. It gives citizens legal tools to challenge inadequate provision of basic services. It requires government to justify its priorities and to show that it is making progress towards realising constitutional commitments. It empowers courts to ensure that marginalised groups are not ignored.

4.16 INCORPORATING THE STRUCTURE: THE JUDICIARY AND ITS ROLE

The Judiciary ensures the rule of law and interprets the Constitution.

- **Independence**: Judges are appointed to safeguard impartiality.
- **Hierarchy**: Includes the High Court, Court of Appeal and Magistrates' Courts.
- **Judicial review**: Courts can strike down laws or actions inconsistent with the Constitution.

The Judiciary is the branch of government responsible for interpreting the law and ensuring that other branches act within constitutional limits. Its independence is essential to its function. Judges must be free from pressure or influence by the Executive, the legislature, or any other actor. They must decide cases according to the law, not according to what is popular or what those in power desire.

Botswana's Judiciary has a strong reputation for independence and integrity. Judges are appointed through processes designed to insulate them from political pressure. They serve with security of tenure, unable to be removed except for cause and through procedures that protect their independence. They have issued decisions against the government when the law required it, and those decisions have been respected.

In *Attorney General v. Dow* (1992), the Judiciary upheld constitutional guarantees of equality, reinforcing its role as guardian of rights. This case is a landmark in Botswana's constitutional jurisprudence. The Court of Appeal struck down a law that discriminated based on sex, holding that such discrimination violated the Constitution's guarantee of fundamental rights. The decision demonstrated the courts' willingness to enforce constitutional limits even against the government, and it established the Judiciary as a genuine check on power.

4.17 INCORPORATING THE STRUCTURE: THE EXECUTIVE AND ACCOUNTABILITY

The Executive branch is headed by the President, who serves as both Head of State and Head of Government.

- **Presidential powers**: Appointing ministers, directing policy and representing Botswana internationally.
- **Cabinet**: Composed of ministers responsible for specific portfolios.
- **Accountability**: The President is elected by the National Assembly and must maintain parliamentary confidence.

The Executive is the branch of government that implements laws and administers public affairs. In Botswana, as in many presidential systems, the Executive is headed by a President who combines the ceremonial functions of Head of State with the governing functions of Head of Government. This concentration of roles gives the President significant visibility and authority.

The President's powers include appointing ministers, directing policy and representing Botswana internationally. These powers are substantial, but they are not unlimited. Ministers are accountable to Parliament and the President must maintain parliamentary confidence. Parliament must approve the Executive's budget. Its actions are subject to judicial review.

The President's role in shaping foreign policy has been critical in positioning Botswana as a respected voice in regional organisations, such as the Southern African Development Community (SADC). This illustrates how Executive power, when exercised responsibly, can serve national interests and enhance the country's standing abroad.

4.18 INCORPORATING THE STRUCTURE: THE LEGISLATURE AND LAW-MAKING

The legislative branch consists of the National Assembly and the House of Chiefs.

- **National Assembly**: Elected representatives debate and pass laws.
- **House of Chiefs**: Provides advisory input, particularly on matters affecting customary law.
- **Law-making process**: Bills are introduced, debated, and passed before receiving presidential assent.

The Legislature is the branch of government that makes laws. In Botswana, the Legislature is bicameral, though the House of Chiefs has advisory rather than legislative powers. The National Assembly, composed of elected representatives, is the primary law-making body.

The law-making process involves multiple stages. Bills are introduced, either by the government or by private members. They are debated in the Assembly, often going through multiple readings. Committees may examine bills in detail, hearing evidence and proposing amendments. Once passed by the Assembly, bills receive presidential assent before becoming law.

This process ensures that legislation is carefully considered. Debates allow different perspectives to be heard. Committee scrutiny allows detailed examination of provisions and their implications. The requirement of presidential assent ensures that the Executive has an opportunity to review legislation before it becomes law, though Parliament can override a presidential veto with a sufficient majority.

Debates on land reform legislation illustrate how the National Assembly balances modern economic needs with traditional land tenure systems. Land is a particularly sensitive issue in Botswana, involving competing claims of economic development, customary rights, and historical justice.

Parliamentary debates on land reform reflect these tensions and the effort to find balanced solutions.

4.19 CONCLUSION

Constitutional democracy in Botswana is founded on the supremacy of the Constitution, the rule of law, separation of powers and protection of fundamental rights. While Botswana has achieved remarkable constitutional stability, continuous reflection and reform are necessary to respond to changing social needs. Strengthening constitutionalism, expanding rights protection, and maintaining accountable governance remain essential for sustaining democracy and preventing abuse of power.

The framework of constitutional democracy is not self-executing. It requires constant effort to maintain and renew. Institutions must be staffed by people committed to constitutional values. Citizens must be educated about their rights and responsibilities. Civil society must monitor government and advocate for accountability. The media must inform the public and expose wrongdoing.

Botswana's constitutional democracy has endured for more than half a century. This is a significant achievement, one that distinguishes it from many other African countries. But endurance does not mean perfection. The limitations identified in this chapter-gaps in the Bill of Rights, concerns about executive dominance, challenges of electoral disproportionality-warrant attention. Constitutional review offers an opportunity to address them, to strengthen the framework of constitutional democracy and to ensure that it continues to serve the people of Botswana for generations to come.

RECAP AND TRANSITION

Recap: This chapter has explored the meaning and components of constitutional democracy. It has distinguished constitutional government from arbitrary government, explained the concept of constitutionalism and its importance, and analysed the rule of law and good governance. It has examined the separation of powers and checks and balances, the role of Parliament, and the Bill of Rights, including its limitations and possibilities for improvement. It has incorporated structural elements from Botswana's Constitution-the Judiciary, the Executive, the Legislature-to show how constitutional democracy operates in practice.

Transition: Having established the framework of constitutional democracy, the structures, principles, and institutions through which government is organised and limited, the next chapter turns to the most direct expression of constitutional limits on government: the protection of fundamental rights. Chapter Five examines in detail how the Constitution of Botswana protects basic rights, analysing each provision of the Bill of Rights and exploring how courts have interpreted and enforced these guarantees. It asks not only what rights the Constitution protects, but also how those rights are given practical effect and what remedies are available when they are violated.

CHAPTER FIVE

HOW DOES THE CONSTITUTION PROTECT OUR BASIC RIGHTS?

5.1 INTRODUCTION

A Bill of Rights is a fundamental component of a democratic constitutional order. It sets out the basic rights and freedoms to which all individuals are entitled, and serves as a limitation on the exercise of state power. The primary purpose of a Bill of Rights is to protect individuals from arbitrary or oppressive actions by the government and to promote human dignity, equality, and freedom under the law. In constitutional democracies, the Bill of Rights functions as both a shield for citizens and a yardstick against which all laws, policies, and governmental actions are measured.

In Botswana, the protection of fundamental human rights is entrenched in **Chapter II of the Constitution**, commonly referred to as the Bill of Rights. Sections 3–18 of the Constitution enumerate and safeguard the basic rights and freedoms of the individual. These provisions are legally enforceable and may be invoked before the courts where a violation is alleged. The Judiciary, particularly the High Court and the Court of Appeal, plays a crucial role in interpreting and enforcing these rights, thereby ensuring constitutional supremacy.

The Bill of Rights is the Constitution's most direct expression of the value of human dignity. It announces that certain things-life, liberty, freedom of expression, protection from discrimination-are so fundamental that they must be protected against even the most popular or well-intentioned government action. These rights are not gifts from the state to the citizen; they are inherent entitlements that the Constitution recognises and secures.

This chapter examines each of the rights protected in Sections 3–18 of Botswana's Constitution. It explains the content of each right, explores how courts have interpreted and applied these provisions, and considers the mechanisms through which rights are enforced. It also examines the relationship between the Bill of Rights and other constitutional provisions, showing how the protection of rights is woven into the broader fabric of constitutional governance.

5.2 SECTION 3: FUNDAMENTAL RIGHTS AND FREEDOMS OF THE INDIVIDUAL

Section 3 serves as the foundational provision of the Bill of Rights. It guarantees every person in Botswana the enjoyment of fundamental rights and freedoms, regardless of race, place of origin, political opinions, colour, creed, or sex. These rights include the right to life, liberty, security of the person, freedom of conscience, expression, assembly, and association, as well as protection of privacy and property.

The importance of Section 3 lies in its recognition of human dignity and equality as core constitutional values. It affirms that these rights are subject only to limitations that are reasonably justifiable in a democratic society.

In **Attorney General v Unity Dow (1992)**, the Court of Appeal affirmed that Section 3 is not merely introductory but has substantive force. The court held that constitutional interpretation must be generous and purposive, especially where fundamental rights are concerned. This case underscored the Constitution's commitment to equality and non-discrimination.

Section 3 is the gateway to the entire Bill of Rights. It announces the rights that the subsequent sections elaborate and protect, and it establishes the principle that these rights belong to every person in Botswana, citizen and non-citizen alike. The reference to "every person in Botswana" is significant: it means that rights protection extends beyond citizens to all who find themselves within the country's jurisdiction.

The enumeration of prohibited grounds of discrimination: race, place of origin, political opinions, colour, creed, or sex, reflects the concerns of Botswana's society at independence. Race and place of origin were central to the colonial experience. Political opinions were sensitive given the Cold War context and the recent transition to independence. Sex was expressly not included until later, when the case of Unity *Dow* ruled that it is impermissible to discriminate based on sex.

The Court of Appeal's decision in *Attorney General v Unity Dow* (1992) was a watershed moment in Botswana's constitutional jurisprudence. The case challenged a provision of the Citizenship Act that denied Botswana citizenship to children of Botswana women married to foreign men, while granting citizenship to children of Botswana men married to foreign women. The government argued that this differentiation was permissible and that Section 3's list of prohibited grounds did not include sex. The Court of Appeal rejected this argument, holding that discrimination based on sex violated the Constitution's guarantee of fundamental rights. The court emphasised that constitutional interpretation must be generous and purposive, not narrow and technical, and that the rights protected in Section 3 must be given full effect.

This decision established several important principles. First, it affirmed that the Bill of Rights protects against discrimination, even on grounds not explicitly listed, if the discrimination is arbitrary or unjustified. Second, it established that courts have the authority to strike down legislation that violates constitutional rights. Third, it demonstrated that the Judiciary would act as a genuine guardian of constitutional values, even against the government of the day.

5.3 SECTION 4: PROTECTION OF THE RIGHT TO LIFE

Section 4 guarantees the right to life and provides that no person shall be intentionally deprived of life, except in execution of a court sentence following conviction for a criminal offence. This section reflects the sanctity of human life and places strict limits on the circumstances under which life may be lawfully taken.

The Constitution further regulates the use of lethal force by state authorities, permitting it only where reasonably necessary, such as in defence of persons or for the suppression of riots or insurrections.

The right to life is fundamental, and any limitation must be strictly construed. The courts have consistently required that any deprivation of life must comply fully with constitutional safeguards.

The right to life is the most fundamental of all rights. Without life, no other rights can be enjoyed. Section 4 recognises this by providing strong protection against intentional deprivation of life by the state or anyone acting on its behalf.

The exception for execution of a court sentence following conviction for a criminal offence reflects the continued existence of the death penalty in Botswana's legal system. This exception has been the subject of debate and litigation, with challenges arguing that the death penalty constitutes cruel, inhuman and degrading treatment prohibited by Section 7. Courts have upheld the constitutionality of the death penalty. Still, they have also imposed strict procedural requirements to ensure that it is imposed only in the most serious cases and after full and fair proceedings.

The regulation of lethal force by state authorities is an important safeguard. Police and other security forces may use lethal force only where reasonably necessary, such as in defence of persons or for the suppression of riots or insurrections. This means that lethal force cannot be used merely to enforce the law or to prevent minor offences. It must be necessary to protect life or to prevent serious violence, and even then, it must be proportionate to the threat.

5.4 SECTION 5: PROTECTION FROM DEPRIVATION OF PERSONAL LIBERTY

Section 5 provides that no person shall be deprived of his or her personal liberty, save as may be authorised by law under circumstances listed in the said section. The exceptions include the execution of a sentence or order of court, and upon reasonable suspicion that a person has committed or is about to commit a criminal offence under the law in force in Botswana.

The right to personal liberty is a cornerstone of constitutional democracy, and any detention must strictly comply with constitutional requirements.

Personal liberty, freedom from arbitrary arrest and detention, is essential to a free society. Without it, all other rights are insecure. A person who can be locked up at will, without charge or trial, cannot exercise freedom of expression, assembly, or association. They cannot practise their religion, pursue their occupation, or participate in public life.

The section also guarantees procedural safeguards. A person who is arrested must be informed promptly of the reasons for arrest. They must be brought before a court within a reasonable time, normally within 48 hours. These safeguards ensure that detention is not secret, that it is subject to judicial oversight, and that the detained person has an opportunity to challenge its lawfulness.

5.5 SECTION 6: PROTECTION FROM SLAVERY AND FORCED LABOUR

Section 6 prohibits slavery, servitude and forced labour. It reflects international human rights norms and Botswana's commitment to eradicating exploitative practices.

The Constitution allows limited exceptions, such as compulsory labour as part of a lawful sentence or service during emergencies. However, these exceptions are narrowly defined to prevent abuse.

Constitutional provisions must be interpreted in a manner that promotes freedom and dignity, reinforcing protections against coercive practices.

Slavery and servitude represent the most extreme forms of domination, in which one person is treated as the property of another. Their prohibition is universal and absolute. No modern Constitution tolerates slavery and international law regards it as a peremptory norm from which no derogation is permitted.

Forced labour is a broader category, encompassing various forms of compelled work. The Constitution prohibits forced labour but allows limited exceptions: labour required as part of a lawful sentence of imprisonment, labour required in emergencies such as fire or flood, and normal civic obligations such as jury service or military service. These exceptions are narrowly drawn and strictly construed, ensuring that they do not become loopholes through which forced labour can be reintroduced.

The prohibition of forced labour has practical implications for labour relations, prison administration, and emergency powers. It means that work cannot be compelled except in the specified circumstances, and even then, the compulsion must be proportionate and respectful of human dignity.

5.5 SECTION 7: PROTECTION FROM INHUMAN TREATMENT

Section 7 protects individuals from torture and from inhuman or degrading punishment or treatment. This right is absolute and non-derogable, meaning it cannot be limited, even in times of emergency.

The courts in Botswana have taken a firm stance against conduct that violates human dignity. In **State v Petrus (1984)**, although predating some later developments, the judiciary affirmed that punishment or treatment that degrades human dignity is unconstitutional.

This provision ensures that law enforcement agencies, prisons, and courts respect the inherent dignity of every individual.

The prohibition of torture and inhuman or degrading treatment is absolute. Unlike many other rights, which may be limited for specified purposes and subject to justification, the right protected in Section 7 admits of no exceptions. Even in times of war, public emergency, or other threat to the nation, torture and inhuman treatment remain prohibited.

This absolutism reflects a fundamental judgement about human dignity. Some things are always wrong, regardless of the circumstances. Torture is one of them. It violates the inherent dignity of the person, degrades those who practice it and undermines the very foundations of a just legal order.

The courts have given effect to this prohibition in various contexts. They have insisted that prison conditions meet minimum standards of humanity. They have required that suspects in police custody be treated with respect and not subjected to violence or intimidation. They have held that punishments must be proportionate to offences and must not degrade the humanity of those punished.

5.6 SECTION 8: PROTECTION FROM DEPRIVATION OF PROPERTY

Section 8 protects individuals from arbitrary deprivation of property. Property may only be compulsorily acquired for public purposes and subject to prompt and adequate compensation.

Property rights protect the material basis of individual autonomy. People need security in their possessions (their homes, their land, their goods) to plan their lives, to invest in the future, to feel safe from arbitrary dispossession.

Section 8 does not make property rights absolute. It recognises that property may need to be acquired for public purposes: to build roads, schools, hospitals, or other infrastructure; to implement land reform; to protect the environment. But such an acquisition must meet strict conditions: it must be for a public purpose; it must be authorised by law; and it must be accompanied by prompt and adequate compensation.

These conditions ensure that the burden of public projects is not unfairly imposed on individuals. Those who lose property for public purposes are entitled to compensation that makes them whole, so that they do not bear a disproportionate share of the cost of public goods.

5.7 SECTION 9: PROTECTION FOR THE PRIVACY OF HOME AND OTHER PROPERTY

Section 9 provides that, except with his or her own consent, no person shall be subjected to the search of his or her person or his or her property, or the entry by others on his or her premises. Exceptions to the above may be made that are reasonably required in the interests of defence, public safety, public morality and public health.

5.8 SECTION 10: PROVISIONS TO SECURE PROTECTION OF THE LAW

Section 10 provides that if any person is charged with a criminal offence, then, unless the charge is withdrawn, the case shall be afforded a fair hearing within a reasonable time, by an independent and impartial court established or recognised by law. The section also provides other rights of a person charged with a criminal offence, such as the presumption of innocence.

5.9 SECTION 11: PROTECTION OF FREEDOM OF CONSCIENCE

Section 11 guarantees freedom of conscience, including freedom of thought, religion, belief and opinion. It also protects the right to manifest one's religion, subject to limitations necessary in the interests of public order and morality.

Our courts often insist that the courts recognised that freedom of conscience includes the right to hold beliefs without interference, and that any restriction must be justified and proportionate.

Freedom of conscience protects the inner realm of belief and thought. It guarantees that individuals may hold whatever religious, philosophical, or moral beliefs they choose, without interference from the state. The state cannot compel belief, cannot punish for belief, and cannot discriminate based on belief.

The right to manifest religion or belief (to worship, to teach, to practice) is also protected, but it may be subject to limitations. Manifestation can affect others in ways that mere belief does not. Public order, safety, health and morality may justify restrictions on religious practice, provided those restrictions are proportionate and not discriminatory.

Freedom of conscience is particularly important in a diverse society like Botswana, where different religious traditions coexist. It ensures that all may practice their faith freely while also protecting those who hold no religious beliefs. It creates space for dialogue and mutual respect among different communities.

5.10 SECTION 12: PROTECTION OF FREEDOM OF EXPRESSION

Section 12 protects freedom of expression, including the freedom to hold opinions and to receive and impart ideas and information. This right is essential for democratic governance and accountability.

The courts often insist that freedom of expression must be broadly interpreted, and that limitations must be reasonably justifiable in a democratic society.

Freedom of expression is the lifeblood of democracy. It enables citizens to discuss public affairs, to criticise government and to advocate for change. It enables the media to inform the public, to investigate wrongdoing and to hold power to account. It enables artists, writers, and scholars to create and to challenge.

Section 12 protects expression in all its forms: spoken and written, artistic and political, individual and collective. It protects the right to hold opinions, even unpopular ones. It protects the right to receive information and ideas, as well as to impart them.

Like other rights, freedom of expression may be limited for specified purposes: defence, public order, morality, reputation, privacy and so on. But limitations must be "reasonably justifiable in a democratic society". This means they must be proportionate, necessary and consistent with democratic values. Restrictions that are excessive, vague or discriminatory will not survive judicial scrutiny.

Freedom of the press has enabled Botswana's media to play a watchdog role, though debates continue about balancing press freedom with national security concerns. This tension is inherent in freedom of expression. Security is important, but it cannot be used as a blanket excuse to suppress criticism or conceal wrongdoing. Courts must carefully scrutinise claims that an expression threatens security, ensuring that restrictions are genuinely necessary and not merely convenient for those in power.

5.12 SECTION 13: PROTECTION OF FREEDOM OF ASSEMBLY AND ASSOCIATION

Section 13 guarantees the right to assemble peacefully and to associate with others, including forming or joining trade unions and political organisations.

In **Botswana Public Employees Union v Minister of Labour (2011)**, the courts recognised the importance of association in protecting workers' rights and democratic participation.

Freedom of assembly allows people to gather together to express shared views, to protest, to celebrate, to mourn. It is essential to social movements, religious communities and political campaigns. Peaceful assembly is protected; assemblies that threaten violence or public order may be restricted, but restrictions must be proportionate and not directed at the content of the views expressed.

Freedom of association allows people to form and join organisations that pursue shared interests. Trade unions, political parties, professional associations, religious groups and many other organisations depend on this right. Association enables collective action, amplifies voices that might otherwise go unheard and provides structures through which people can participate in public life.

The *Botswana Public Employees Union* case recognised the importance of association for workers. Trade unions enable employees to bargain collectively with employers, to advocate for better wages and working conditions and to protect their members' interests. Without freedom of association, workers would face employers individually, with vastly unequal power.

5.13 SECTION 14: PROTECTION OF FREEDOM OF MOVEMENT

Section 14 protects the right to move freely throughout Botswana, to reside in any part of the country, and to leave and return. Restrictions are permitted only where necessary in the public interest. Freedom of movement is central to personal autonomy and identity.

Freedom of movement enables people to live where they choose, to travel for work or leisure, to visit family and friends, and to seek opportunities beyond their home communities. It is essential to personal autonomy and to the functioning of a modern economy.

The right to leave and return to Botswana is particularly important. It means that citizens cannot be trapped in the country against their will and that those who leave retain the right to come back. This protects against exile and banishment, practices that authoritarian regimes have used to silence opponents.

Restrictions on movement may be imposed in the public interest, for example, to control infectious diseases, to protect the environment, or to maintain public order. But such restrictions must be necessary and proportionate. Blanket restrictions that the circumstances cannot justify will be struck down.

5.14 SECTION 15: PROTECTION FROM DISCRIMINATION

Section 15 prohibits discriminatory laws or practices on grounds such as race, tribe, place of origin, political opinion, colour or creed.

In **Attorney General v Unity Dow**, the Court of Appeal held that discrimination based on gender violated constitutional guarantees, marking a landmark advancement in equality jurisprudence.

Section 15 is the Constitution's primary equality guarantee. It prohibits laws and practices that discriminate on specified grounds. Discrimination means treating people differently in ways that are arbitrary or unjust, that impose burdens or deny benefits without good reason.

The listed grounds-race, tribe, place of origin, political opinion, colour, creed-reflect the particular concerns of Botswana's society at independence. But as *Unity Dow* established, the prohibition of discrimination is not limited to these grounds. Discrimination on other grounds, such as sex, may also violate the Constitution if it is arbitrary and unjustified.

Unity Dow was significant precisely because it extended constitutional protection to a ground, sex, not explicitly mentioned in Section 15. The court held that the Constitution's commitment to fundamental rights and freedoms, expressed in Section 3, prohibited discrimination on grounds of sex, even if Section 15 did not explicitly say so. This interpretation gave the Constitution a dynamic and evolving character, enabling it to address new understandings of equality and justice.

5.15 SECTIONS 16–18: ENFORCEMENT, INTERPRETATION, AND EXCEPTIONS

These sections provide mechanisms for enforcement of rights, interpretation of limitations and exceptions during emergencies. Section 18 empowers the High Court to hear constitutional matters, ensuring access to justice.

The courts are guardians of the Constitution and must provide effective remedies for violations.

Rights are meaningful only if they can be enforced. Sections 16–18 provide the mechanisms through which individuals can vindicate their constitutional rights.

Section 16 deals with interpretation. It provides that limitations on rights must be interpreted restrictively, and that rights themselves must be interpreted generously. This interpretive direction shapes how courts approach constitutional cases.

Section 17 allows for derogations from certain rights during periods of public emergency. But even during emergencies, some rights, such as protection from torture, remain absolute. And any derogation must be proportionate to the threat and must not discriminate arbitrarily.

Section 18 is perhaps the most important enforcement provision. It gives the High Court original jurisdiction to hear constitutional matters. Any person who alleges that their rights have been violated can apply to the High Court for relief. The court has the power to issue remedies-declarations, injunctions, damages-to vindicate rights and remedy violations.

Access to court is essential. Rights that cannot be invoked in court are not rights at all. Section 18 ensures that every person in Botswana has a judicial remedy for violations of their constitutional rights.

5.16 INCORPORATING THE STRUCTURE: FUNDAMENTAL RIGHTS AND FREEDOMS

The Constitution guarantees a wide range of rights:

- **Civil liberties**: Freedom of speech, assembly, and association
- **Equality**: Protection against discrimination
- **Due process**: Right to a fair trial and protection from arbitrary detention

The Bill of Rights protects both negative and positive dimensions of freedom. Negatively, it protects against state interference: freedom from censorship, from arbitrary arrest, from discrimination. Positively, it creates conditions for participation: freedom to speak, to assemble, to associate, to move.

Due process rights are particularly important. They ensure that when the state does act against individuals, through criminal prosecution, deportation, or other coercive measures, it must follow fair procedures. The right to a fair trial includes the right to be heard, to present evidence, to confront witnesses, to have legal representation, and to appeal. These safeguards protect against miscarriages of justice and ensure that state power is exercised fairly.

5.17 INCORPORATING THE STRUCTURE: CUSTOMARY LAW AND RIGHTS

Botswana's Constitution recognises customary law and traditional leadership.

- **House of Chiefs**: Advises on issues affecting customary practices.
- **Customary Courts**: Resolve disputes at community level.
- **Integration**: Customary law operates alongside statutory law, provided it does not conflict with constitutional principles.

The relationship between customary law and constitutional rights is complex and sometimes contested. Customary law reflects the traditions and values of communities, developed over generations to govern social relations, resolve disputes and allocate resources. Constitutional rights reflect universal norms of human dignity and equality, developed through international human rights instruments and comparative constitutional practice.

When customary law conflicts with constitutional rights, the Constitution prevails. This is fundamental to constitutional supremacy. But the resolution of conflicts need not always involve displacing customary law entirely. Sometimes, customary rules can be interpreted and applied in ways that respect constitutional values. Sometimes, customary institutions can be adapted to give effect to rights. Sometimes, dialogue between customary and constitutional norms can produce creative solutions that honour both.

Disputes over land allocation often involve Customary Courts, highlighting the Constitution's role in harmonising traditional and modern governance. Land is a particularly sensitive area, involving competing claims of customary tenure, statutory title, and constitutional rights. Navigating these competing claims requires careful attention to both legal frameworks and the lived realities of

5.18 THE ROLE OF COURTS IN PROTECTING RIGHTS

The courts play a crucial role in protecting constitutional rights. Through judicial review, they ensure that legislation and executive action comply with constitutional requirements. Through interpretation, they give meaning to constitutional provisions, adapting them to new circumstances and challenges. Through remedies, they provide redress for violations and deter future abuses.

The independence of the judiciary is essential to this role. Judges must be free from pressure or influence by the Executive, the Legislature, or any other actor. They must decide cases according to the law, not according to what is popular or what those in power desire. Security of tenure, financial independence and impartial appointment processes help secure this independence.

The courts have shown themselves willing to play this role. In cases ranging from *Unity Dow* to *Botswana Public Employees Union*, they have enforced constitutional rights against the government. They have struck down legislation, invalidated executive action and ordered remedies for violations. They have given practical effect to the Constitution's promises.

5.19 CONCLUSION

The Constitution of Botswana provides robust protection for fundamental human rights through the Bill of Rights enshrined in Chapter II. Sections 3 to 18 collectively safeguard individual freedoms, limit governmental power, and promote democratic values. Through judicial interpretation, particularly by the Court of Appeal, these rights have been given practical meaning and enforceability. The Constitution, therefore, stands as a living instrument that protects the dignity, liberty, and equality of all persons in Botswana.

The Bill of Rights is the Constitution's most direct expression of the value of human dignity. It announces that certain things are so fundamental that they must be protected against even the most popular or well-intentioned government action. It provides a shield for individuals against the power of the state, and a sword for challenging violations when they occur.

But a Bill of Rights, however well-drafted, is not self-executing. It depends on institutions: courts, legislatures, executives, civil society, etc., to give it effect. It depends on a culture of respect for rights, among officials and citizens alike. It depends on vigilance, on willingness to challenge violations, on commitment to the values it enshrines.

Botswana's Bill of Rights has served the nation well for more than half a century, but it is not perfect. The limitations identified in this chapter-gaps in protection, constraints on enforcement, tensions with customary law-warrant attention. Constitutional review offers an opportunity to address these limitations, to strengthen rights protection, and to ensure that the Constitution continues to serve the people of Botswana for generations to come.

RECAP AND TRANSITION

Recap: This chapter has provided a detailed examination of the Bill of Rights in Botswana's Constitution. It has analysed each of Sections 3–18, explaining the content of each right, exploring judicial interpretations, and considering the mechanisms through which rights are enforced. It has examined the foundational role of Section 3, the protection of specific rights-life, freedom from inhuman treatment, liberty, conscience, expression, assembly, movement, property, privacy, and equality-and the enforcement provisions in Sections 16-18. It has also considered the relationship between constitutional rights and customary law and the role of courts in protecting rights.

Transition: Having examined the specific rights protected in Botswana's Constitution and the mechanisms for their enforcement, Part 1 now turns to a deeper theoretical question: What makes a constitutional order genuinely constitutional? The next chapter explores the concept of **constitutionalism**: the principles and practices that ensure government power is exercised within constitutional limits, that rights are respected, and that those who govern remain accountable to those who are governed. Chapter Six explains why a Constitution on paper is not enough and what it takes to make constitutionalism a living reality.

Chapter Six

CONSTITUTIONALISM – THE SOUL OF A CONSTITUTIONAL ORDER

6.1 INTRODUCTION

A Constitution is often described as the supreme law of the land, a document that establishes the framework of government and guarantees the rights of citizens. Yet, the mere existence of a written Constitution does not guarantee that a country is governed democratically or that the rights of individuals are respected. History provides many examples of regimes that operated under constitutions while ruling arbitrarily, suppressing dissent, and violating fundamental freedoms.

What distinguishes a genuine constitutional democracy from a system that merely possesses a Constitution is a deeper set of principles and practices. That deeper framework is **constitutionalism**. Constitutionalism is a complex and multifaceted concept that extends beyond the mere existence of a constitution. It encompasses the principles and practices that ensure the exercise of government power is conducted in a manner consistent with fundamental norms and values, such as the rule of law, democracy and human rights.

This chapter explores the meaning of constitutionalism, its essential components, and its significance for Botswana's constitutional order. It draws on scholarly perspectives to explain why constitutionalism is not merely an abstract ideal but a practical necessity for limiting government power and protecting the dignity of citizens. It also examines how constitutionalism operates in Botswana, considering both strengths and areas where further development may be needed.

The distinction between a Constitution and constitutionalism is fundamental. A Constitution is a text; constitutionalism is a practice. A constitution can be written in a day; constitutionalism takes generations to develop. A ruler can impose a Constitution; constitutionalism must be embraced by a society. A Constitution without constitutionalism is like a body without breath-it has form but not life.

6.2 DEFINING CONSTITUTIONALISM

At its core, constitutionalism refers to **the practice and process of government being bound by and operating within a framework of laws and principles set out in a Constitution**.

This definition emphasises several key elements. First, constitutionalism is a **practice and process**, not merely a set of rules. It is about how government actually operates, day by day, year by year. It is about the habits, attitudes, and behaviours of officials and citizens. It is about what happens when constitutional rules are tested by political crisis or administrative convenience.

Second, constitutionalism requires that government be **bound by** law. This means that legal limits are real and effective. Officials cannot simply ignore them when they become inconvenient. Courts can enforce them against those who would transgress. Citizens can invoke them to challenge governmental action.

Third, constitutionalism requires that government operate **within a framework** of laws and principles. This framework is not just any laws, but the fundamental laws set out in the Constitution. The Constitution is the touchstone against which all governmental action is measured.

Constitutionalism involves the following key components:

- Rule of Law
- Separation of powers
- Protection of fundamental rights

- Public accountability
- Transparency
- Power of judicial review

Each of these components contributes to the overall project of limited, accountable government. Together, they form the architecture of constitutionalism. None is sufficient alone; all are necessary. A system that has separation of powers, but no protection of rights, may still be tyrannical. A system that protects rights on paper but has no independent Judiciary to enforce them may leave rights vulnerable. Constitutionalism requires the whole ensemble to work together.

6.3 KEY COMPONENTS OF CONSTITUTIONALISM

6.3.1 The Rule of Law

Rule of Law: Government actions must be based on and constrained by law. This implies legality, predictability, and fairness in the exercise of public power.

The rule of law is the foundation upon which all other components of constitutionalism rest. It means that law, not will, governs. Decisions are made according to pre-announced rules, not according to the whim of officials. Those rules apply equally to all, not differently to favourites and disfavours. And they are enforced by courts that are independent of those who make and execute the laws.

In Botswana, the rule of law is reflected in the Constitution's structure and in the independence of the Judiciary. Courts have consistently affirmed that the government must act within the bounds set by law, and that citizens have enforceable rights when those bounds are exceeded. The principle that no one is above the law (not the President, not Parliament, not the military) is deeply embedded in Botswana's legal culture.

The rule of law has both formal and substantive dimensions. Formally, it requires that laws be clear, public, stable, and applied generally. Substantively, it requires that laws respect fundamental rights and human dignity. A system that clearly and consistently applies oppressive laws would satisfy the formal rule of law but violate its substantive dimension. Modern understandings of constitutionalism encompass both aspects: law must be both properly enacted and fundamentally just.

6.3.2 Separation of Powers

Separation of Powers: Constitutionalism requires a division of government into distinct branches (legislative, executive, and judicial) to prevent the concentration of power and to provide checks and balances.

The separation of powers is a structural response to the problem of concentrated power. If all power is gathered in one place, those who hold it are tempted to abuse it. They make the laws, execute them, and judge their application, all without any external check. History teaches that such concentration leads to tyranny.

The separation of powers disperses authority among different branches, each with its own functions and each capable of checking the others. The Legislature makes the laws, but the Executive implements them, and the Judiciary interprets them. The Executive administers the government, but the Legislature funds it, and the Judiciary reviews its actions. The Judiciary decides cases, but its members are appointed by the Executive and confirmed by the Legislature, and its decisions can prompt legislative revision.

In Botswana, although the Constitution does not explicitly mention separation of powers, the courts have pronounced that separation of powers is implicit in the Constitution and have given it effect in their decisions. Each branch operates with a degree of independence, and each respects the proper sphere of the others.

6.3.3 Protection of Fundamental Rights

Protection of Fundamental Rights: Constitutions often enshrine human rights and fundamental freedoms, which the government is obligated to protect and uphold.

A Bill of Rights is the Constitution's most direct expression of the limits on governmental power. It announces that certain things-life, liberty, freedom of expression, equality-are so fundamental that they must be protected against even the most popular or well-intentioned government action. These rights are not gifts from the state to the citizen; they are inherent entitlements that the Constitution recognises and secures.

Chapter II of Botswana's Constitution guarantees a range of fundamental rights, including the right to life, protection from inhuman treatment, freedom of expression, freedom of assembly and association, protection from discrimination, and many others. These rights are enforceable through the courts, and the Judiciary has shown itself willing to give them practical effect.

The protection of rights is not merely a matter of having a Bill of Rights. It requires that rights be taken seriously by all branches of government, that courts have the authority and willingness to enforce them, and that citizens know their rights and can claim them. It requires a culture of respect for rights that permeates the entire society.

6.3.4 Accountability and Transparency

Accountability and Transparency: Public officials are accountable to the law and to the citizens. Decisions must be transparent, and there must be mechanisms for holding officials responsible for their actions.

Accountability means that officials must answer for their actions. They must explain their decisions, justify their use of resources and accept consequences when they fail. Accountability operates through multiple channels: elections, parliamentary oversight, judicial review, media scrutiny and civil society advocacy. Each channel provides a different mechanism for holding power to account.

Transparency means that government operates openly. Citizens can see what their government is doing, understand how decisions are made and access information about public affairs. Transparency enables accountability by providing the information citizens need to judge their government's performance. It also builds trust by demonstrating that government has nothing to hide.

In Botswana, parliamentary oversight, independent institutions such as the Office of the Ombudsman, and a free media contribute to accountability and transparency. The Ombudsman's investigations into administrative misconduct demonstrate how independent institutions can protect citizens from abuse. The media's watchdog role helps expose wrongdoing and inform public debate.

6.3.5 Judicial Review

Judicial Review: Courts have the power to review and, if necessary, nullify government actions that violate the Constitution. This ensures that all branches of government act within constitutional limits.

Judicial review is the mechanism through which constitutional limits are enforced. Without it, constitutional provisions would be mere exhortations, lacking binding force. A Legislature that passed unconstitutional laws could do so with impunity. An Executive who violated constitutional rights could act without consequence. The Constitution would be what those in power said it was, not a genuine limit on their authority.

Judicial review empowers courts to strike down laws and actions that violate the Constitution. This is a powerful check on both legislative and executive power. It ensures that, even when political actors have majority support, they cannot override constitutional limits. It gives individuals a forum in which to challenge governmental action and obtain remedies for violations.

Botswana's High Court and Court of Appeal exercise this power, declaring legislation or executive action invalid when it conflicts with the Constitution. The landmark case of *Attorney General v Unity Dow* (1992) exemplifies this function, with the Court of Appeal striking down a law that discriminated based on sex, affirming that the Constitution protects all persons equally.

6.4 SCHOLARLY PERSPECTIVES ON CONSTITUTIONALISM

The presentation draws on several influential thinkers, whose work has shaped modern understandings of constitutionalism.

6.4.1 Locke and Montesquieu

John Locke and Montesquieu are often cited as early proponents of constitutionalism, advocating for the separation of powers and the idea that government must be conducted according to established laws.

Locke's theory of government by consent laid the groundwork for constitutionalism. He argued that legitimate government arises from the consent of the governed and is limited by the purposes for which it was created. Government exists to protect natural rights: life, liberty, and property; and when it acts against those ends, it exceeds its authority. This understanding of limited government, founded on consent and directed toward the protection of rights, is fundamental to constitutionalism.

Montesquieu developed the theory of separation of powers that has influenced constitutional design worldwide. He argued that liberty is threatened when legislative, executive, and judicial powers are combined in the same person or body. By separating these powers and giving each the capacity to check the others, a Constitution can protect liberty even in a large and complex state. His ideas shaped the design of many Constitutions, including those of the United States, France, and the many countries that followed their examples.

6.4.2 Albert Venn Dicey

Albert Venn Dicey emphasised the rule of law as a cornerstone of constitutionalism, highlighting that no person is above the law and that all are subject to the same legal standards.

Dicey's formulation of the rule of law remains influential. He identified three core elements: the absolute supremacy of regular law as opposed to arbitrary power; equality before the law, with all persons subject to the same legal standards and the same courts; and the protection of rights through ordinary legal remedies rather than through abstract declarations. For Dicey, the rule of law meant that government could act only through law, that officials were as subject to law as ordinary citizens, and that rights were secure because they could be enforced in court.

Dicey's emphasis on legal remedies rather than abstract declarations is particularly important. It reminds us that rights are meaningful only when they can be enforced. A Bill of Rights that cannot be invoked in court is not a protection, but a pretence. Constitutionalism requires not only that rights be declared, but that there be mechanisms for their enforcement.

6.4.3 Charles Howard McIlwain

Charles Howard McIlwain articulated that constitutionalism involves the limitation of government power, which must be exercised within the bounds of fundamental principles.

For McIlwain, the essence of constitutionalism lies in restraint. Government is legitimate only when it operates within boundaries set by law and principle. These boundaries are not merely procedural; they reflect fundamental values that cannot be overridden even by majorities. Constitutionalism thus stands in opposition to the idea of unlimited sovereignty, whether of a monarch or of a parliament.

McIlwain's emphasis on fundamental principles is important. It recognises that constitutionalism is not just about following procedures, but about respecting substantive values. A government that followed all the proper procedures to enact oppressive laws might be legal, but it would not be constitutional in the deeper sense. Constitutionalism requires that law be both properly enacted and fundamentally just.

6.4.4 David Feldman

More recently, David Feldman noted that constitutionalism encompasses both the formal legal structure and the cultural and political practices that ensure the effective operation of constitutional governance.

Feldman's contribution is to emphasise the cultural dimension of constitutionalism. A Constitution may be perfectly designed on paper, but if it is not supported by a culture of respect for constitutional limits, it will fail in practice. Officials must internalise constitutional values, not merely comply with them out of fear of sanctions. Citizens must understand and claim their constitutional rights. Civil society must monitor government and advocate for accountability. The media must inform the public and expose wrongdoing.

This cultural dimension is often overlooked but is essential to constitutionalism's success. It explains why countries with similar constitutional texts can have very different constitutional practices. The difference lies in the culture-the habits, attitudes, and expectations of officials and citizens. Constitutionalism requires not only good institutions, but also a people committed to making those institutions work.

6.5 CONSTITUTIONALISM IN THE BOTSWANA CONTEXT

Botswana's record on constitutionalism is generally strong, but it is not without challenges. Examining each component of constitutionalism in the Botswana context reveals both achievements and areas for continued attention.

6.5.1 Rule of Law in Botswana

The rule of law is well established in Botswana. Courts are independent and respected. Their decisions are obeyed, even when they go against the government. Due process is generally observed in criminal and civil proceedings. Access to justice, while not perfect, is better than in many comparable countries.

However, challenges remain. Delays in the court system can undermine access to justice. The cost of litigation can exclude ordinary citizens. Enforcement of court orders can sometimes be slow or ineffective. And there are concerns about the treatment of marginalised groups, such as the San (Basarwa) communities, whose rights have sometimes been neglected.

6.5.2 Separation of Powers in Botswana

The separation of powers is implicit in Botswana's Constitution and has been recognised by the courts. Each branch operates with a degree of independence, and there is general respect for the proper spheres of each.

But concerns about Executive dominance have been raised. The President holds significant power, combining the roles of Head of State and Head of Government. The Executive's control over the legislative agenda and its dominance in Parliament can weaken oversight. The appointment process for Judges, while generally respected, has been criticised for insufficient transparency.

6.5.3 Protection of Fundamental Rights in Botswana

Botswana's Bill of Rights provides strong protection for civil and political rights. The courts have enforced these rights vigorously, as seen in cases like *Unity Dow* and *Botswana Public Employees Union.*

However, as noted in Chapter Five, there are gaps. Socio-economic rights (to health, education, housing, and social security) are not explicitly protected. Environmental rights are absent. Protection against discrimination could be strengthened by explicitly including additional grounds, such as disability, HIV status and sexual orientation. And limitation clauses, while necessary, can sometimes be applied too broadly.

6.5.4 Accountability and Transparency in Botswana

Botswana has strong institutions of accountability: an independent Judiciary, a free media, an Office of the Ombudsman, an Auditor General, and a vibrant civil society. Elections are held regularly and are generally free and fair.

But concerns persist. The dominance of the Executive can weaken parliamentary oversight. Access to information is not always easy; Botswana lacks a comprehensive freedom of information law. Whistleblower protections are weak, and there are periodic concerns about corruption and the misuse of public funds.

6.5.5 Judicial Review in Botswana

Judicial review is firmly established in Botswana. Courts have the power to strike down laws and actions that violate the Constitution, and they have exercised this power when necessary. The *Unity Dow* case is the most famous example, but there are many others.

The independence of the Judiciary is generally respected. Judges are appointed through processes designed to insulate them from political pressure. They serve with security of tenure and cannot be removed except for cause and through procedures that protect their independence.

6.6 THE RELATIONSHIP BETWEEN CONSTITUTION AND CONSTITUTIONALISM

The presentation's diagram illustrates the relationship between the constitution and constitutionalism:

- **Constitution** provides the **legal framework** and **constitutional principles.**
- **Constitutionalism** is the **practice** and **process** of government being bound by, and operating within, that framework.
- **Constitutionalism** involves key components: **rule of law, separation of powers, protection of fundamental rights, public accountability, transparency, and the power of judicial review.**

This relationship is symbiotic. A Constitution provides the framework within which constitutionalism operates. It establishes institutions, allocates powers, and declares rights. But constitutionalism brings that framework to life. It ensures that institutions actually function as designed, that powers are limited, and that rights are actually protected.

A Constitution without constitutionalism is a dead letter. It may exist on paper, but it does not constrain power in practice. Officials ignore it when convenient. Courts cannot enforce it against powerful interests. Citizens cannot rely on it to protect their rights. The Constitution becomes what those in power say it is, not a genuine limit on their authority.

Constitutionalism without a Constitution is possible in theory-Britain has managed with an unwritten Constitution for centuries—but it is rare and difficult. A written constitution provides clarity, stability, and a focal point for public expectations. It makes constitutional principles visible and accessible. It provides a text that citizens can invoke, and courts can enforce.

6.7 WHY CONSTITUTIONALISM MATTERS

Constitutionalism matters because power corrupts. Those who hold power are tempted to abuse it, to use it for private gain rather than public good, to extend it beyond its proper bounds. Constitutionalism creates mechanisms to resist these temptations. It disperses power so that no single actor can dominate. It establishes limits that even the most powerful must respect. It provides remedies for those whose rights are violated.

Constitutionalism matters because it protects minorities. In a pure democracy, the majority could vote to oppress the minority. Constitutionalism prevents this by establishing fundamental rights that cannot be overridden by majority vote. It ensures that even unpopular groups are protected from persecution.

Constitutionalism matters because it provides stability. When power is exercised according to known rules, people can plan their lives with confidence. They know what to expect from government. They know that their rights will be respected. This predictability enables economic development, social cooperation and peaceful political change.

Constitutionalism matters because it legitimises government. People obey laws not only because they fear punishment, but because they accept the authority of the law. This acceptance depends on the belief that law is made and applied fairly, that it binds rulers as well as ruled, and that it serves the common good rather than private interests. Constitutionalism fosters this belief by demonstrating that government itself is subject to law.

6.8 CHALLENGES TO CONSTITUTIONALISM

Constitutionalism faces challenges in every society, including Botswana. Understanding these challenges is essential to addressing them.

Complacency is a challenge. When constitutionalism has worked well for a long time, people may take it for granted. They may assume that rights will always be protected, that institutions will always function, and that limits will always be respected. This complacency can lead to neglect, allowing constitutionalism to erode gradually.

Executive overreach is a perennial challenge. Executives have advantages in information, initiative, and resources. They can act quickly while Legislatures deliberate slowly. They can frame issues and set agendas. Over time, these advantages can lead to a shift in the balance of power, with the Executive increasingly dominating and checks and balances weakening.

Corruption undermines constitutionalism by creating alternative centres of power that operate outside legal frameworks. When officials can be bought, when bribes can influence decisions, and when public resources can be diverted to private use, the rule of law is weakened and accountability is undermined.

Public apathy is a challenge. Constitutionalism depends on citizens who are informed, engaged, and willing to defend their rights. When citizens are apathetic, when they do not vote, when they do not participate in public life, when they do not challenge abuses, constitutionalism weakens.

Polarisation threatens constitutionalism by eroding the common ground on which constitutional government depends. When society is deeply divided, when each side sees the other as illegitimate, when compromise is seen as betrayal, constitutional institutions come under strain. Courts are attacked, Legislatures are paralysed and Executives act unilaterally.

6.9 INCORPORATING THE STRUCTURE: CHECKS AND BALANCES AS CONSTITUTIONALISM IN ACTION

The Constitution establishes mechanisms to prevent abuse of power:

- **Parliamentary oversight**: Ministers are accountable to the National Assembly.
- **Judicial review**: Courts can invalidate unconstitutional actions.
- **Independent institutions**: Bodies such as the Ombudsman provide additional safeguards.

These mechanisms are concrete expressions of constitutionalism. They give practical effect to the principles of accountability, transparency and limited government. They create multiple channels through which power can be checked and abuses can be corrected.

Parliamentary oversight ensures that the Executive is regularly called to account. Ministers must answer questions, defend their decisions, and justify their use of public resources. This scrutiny, conducted in public, reinforces the principle that power is delegated, not owned.

Judicial review empowers courts to strike down actions that violate the Constitution. This is a powerful check on both legislative and executive power. It ensures that even when political actors have majority support, they cannot override constitutional limits. It gives individuals a forum in which to challenge governmental action and obtain remedies for violations.

Independent institutions like the Ombudsman, the Auditor General and the Independent Electoral Commission serve as guardians of integrity. They operate outside the normal chain of command, reporting directly to Parliament or the public. Their independence allows them to investigate wrongdoing without fear or favour, strengthening accountability and public trust.

6.10 SUSTAINING CONSTITUTIONALISM

Constitutionalism is not permanently secured. It requires constant effort to maintain and renew. Institutions must be staffed by people committed to constitutional values. Citizens must be educated about their rights and responsibilities. Civil society must monitor government and advocate for accountability. The media must inform the public and expose wrongdoing.

Constitutional literacy is essential. Citizens cannot defend their rights if they do not know what those rights are. They cannot hold government accountable if they do not understand how government is supposed to work. Constitutional education, in schools and in the broader society, is an investment in constitutionalism's future.

Vigilance is required. Abuses often begin small, a minor overreach here, a slight restriction there, and gradually accumulate. Citizens and institutions must be alert to these incremental erosions and must resist them before they become entrenched.

Renewal is necessary. Constitutions must adapt to changing circumstances. New challenges emerge that the framers could not have anticipated. New understandings of rights develop. Constitutional amendment and review, when conducted properly, allow constitutions to evolve while maintaining their fundamental commitments.

6.11 CONCLUSION

Constitutionalism is the soul of a constitutional order. It is what transforms a mere document into a living framework for limited, accountable government. It is what ensures that power is exercised according to law, that rights are protected, and that those who govern remain answerable to those who are governed.

The key components of constitutionalism-the rule of law, separation of powers, protection of fundamental rights, accountability, transparency, and judicial review-work together to create a system in which power is both effective and constrained. They reflect insights developed over centuries of political thought and practice, from Locke and Montesquieu to Dicey, McIlwain, and Feldman.

Botswana has made significant progress in building constitutionalism. Its courts are independent, its elections are regular, and its institutions generally function. But constitutionalism is never complete. It requires constant attention, constant effort, constant renewal. The challenges of executive dominance, rights protection, accountability, and transparency require ongoing engagement.

Constitutional review offers an opportunity to strengthen constitutionalism in Botswana. By addressing gaps in rights protection, by strengthening checks and balances, by enhancing accountability mechanisms, and by deepening constitutional literacy, review can renew and deepen the constitutional order. But the review itself must be conducted according to constitutionalist principles: transparently, inclusively, and accountably. The process must reflect the values it seeks to embed.

Ultimately, constitutionalism depends on the people. It is citizens who must claim their rights, who must hold their government accountable, who must defend constitutional limits against overreach. A Constitution can provide the framework, but only a people committed to constitutionalism can give it life.

RECAP AND TRANSITION

Recap: This chapter has explored the concept of constitutionalism-the principles and practices that ensure government power is exercised within constitutional limits. It has defined constitutionalism and distinguished it from the mere existence of a Constitution. It has examined its key components: the rule of law, separation of powers, protection of fundamental rights, accountability, transparency and judicial review. It has drawn on scholarly perspectives from Locke, Montesquieu, Dicey, McIlwain and Feldman to illuminate different dimensions of constitutionalism. It has considered how constitutionalism operates in Botswana, identifying both strengths and challenges. And it has reflected on what sustains constitutionalism over time: constitutional literacy, vigilance, and renewal.

Transition: This chapter concludes Part 1 of the book. Part 1 has examined the foundations of Botswana's constitutional order: its history, its philosophical underpinnings in popular sovereignty and social contract, its republican character, its framework of constitutional democracy, its protection of fundamental rights and its commitment to constitutionalism. These foundations provide the context for understanding why constitutional review matters and what it should seek to achieve.

Part 2 turns to the process of constitutional review itself. It begins with a chapter that explains why process matters as much as content-why how a Constitution is reviewed is as important as what changes are made. It then proceeds through the stages of review, from preliminary questions and guiding principles, through preparation, consultation, analysis, drafting and adoption. It concludes with reflections on how to ensure that constitutional review strengthens rather than weakens Botswana's constitutional order.

PART II

AN OVERVIEW OF THE CONSTITUTIONAL REVIEW PROCESS

Chapter Seven

PROCESS IS AS IMPORTANT AS CONTENT IN CONSTITUTIONAL REVIEW

7.1 INTRODUCTION

Constitutions are often treated as texts: collections of rules, rights, and institutional arrangements. Yet, constitutional experience across the world, including in Africa, demonstrates that how a Constitution is made can be just as important as what it contains.

A Constitution that is technically sound, but born through exclusion, secrecy or elite bargaining, may struggle for legitimacy, compliance and endurance.

The United Nations, the International Institute for Democracy and Electoral Assistance (IDEA), and constitutional scholars consistently emphasise that constitution-making is not merely a legal exercise, but a deeply political and social process. As I often emphasise, Constitutions derive their authority not only from legal validity, but from popular ownership and participation.

This chapter introduces the idea that process equals legitimacy, explores the concept of conversational constitutionalism and explains why Botswana's constitutional review must be approached as a national dialogue, not a technocratic amendment exercise.

The tendency to focus on constitutional content (on the specific provisions, the precise wording, the institutional designs) is understandable. Content is tangible. It can be debated, drafted and defended. It appears in black and white, available for scrutiny and interpretation. Process, by contrast, is ephemeral. It consists of meetings, consultations, negotiations and decisions that may not leave visible traces in the final document.

Yet, the process leaves its mark in less visible but equally important ways. It shapes how citizens perceive the Constitution, whether they see it as theirs or as something imposed on them. It shapes how officials behave, whether they feel bound by constitutional limits or free to ignore them. It shapes how the Constitution endures, whether it can withstand crises and challenges or crumbles at the first sign of stress.

This chapter argues that for Botswana's constitutional review to succeed, the process must be given the same attention as the content. The review must be designed not merely to produce a document, but to build legitimacy, to educate citizens, to foster dialogue, and to create a sense of shared ownership. Only then can the resulting Constitution claim the allegiance of the people it governs.

7.2 CONSTITUTION-MAKING AS A DEMOCRATIC MOMENT

7.2.1 Constitutions as Social Compacts

At its core, a Constitution represents a social compact: an agreement among the people on how they will govern themselves, distribute power, protect rights and resolve conflict. Because this compact binds current and future generations, it demands broad consent.

UN constitutional guidance emphasises that constitutions gain authority when they are perceived as:

- Reflecting the will of the people
- Responding to lived realities
- Offering fair rules for political competition

Where these conditions are absent, Constitutions risk becoming elite pacts, disconnected from society.

The idea of a social compact, explored in Part 1, has direct implications for constitutional review. If the Constitution is a compact among the people, then the people must be parties to its formation. They cannot be bound by an agreement they had no hand in making. This is why process matters: it is through participation that the people become parties to the compact.

The UN guidance identifies three conditions for constitutional authority. First, the Constitution must reflect the will of the people. This does not mean that every provision must command unanimous support, but that the overall framework must be one that the people, through some meaningful process of consent, have endorsed. Second, it must respond to lived realities. A Constitution that ignores the actual conditions of people's lives-their poverty, their aspirations, their conflicts-will be irrelevant at best and oppressive at worst. Third, it must offer fair rules for political competition. The Constitution structures the power struggle; if the rules are seen as rigged in favour of incumbents or elites, they will lack legitimacy.

When these conditions are absent, the Constitution becomes an elite pact. It may serve the interests of those who negotiated it, but it will not command the allegiance of the broader population. Such Constitutions are fragile, vulnerable to rejection when political crises arise.

7.2.2 Important Historical Context

Botswana's 1966 Constitution was negotiated in a colonial context, without popular participation. While it provided stability and institutional continuity, it did not emerge from a broad-based public conversation. Over time, social, economic and political changes (including evolving understandings of human rights, identity, and equality) have created pressure for review.

The circumstances of Botswana's independence Constitution are not unique. Many post-colonial Constitutions were negotiated between colonial powers and local elites, with little or no input from ordinary people. The focus was on achieving independence quickly and establishing functional institutions, not on building popular ownership. These Constitutions often served their immediate purpose, providing frameworks for stability and continuity. But they carried a legitimacy deficit from birth.

Over the decades since independence, this deficit has become more apparent. Understandings of human rights have deepened. Expectations of democratic participation have risen. New social movements have emerged, demanding recognition and inclusion. The Constitution that served Botswana well in its first decades now faces pressure to evolve, to reflect changed circumstances and deepened commitments.

In 2021, the former President of Botswana, Mokgweetsi Masisi, established the Dibotelo Commission under the Commissions of Inquiry Act. This Act empowers the President to appoint commissions to investigate matters of public concern and report findings. This was the wrong Act to invoke to initiate a constitutional review exercise, as the Act is designed for fact-finding investigations (corruption, scandals, administrative failures) rather than participatory constitutional reform. There are five main reasons why the Act was inappropriate:

(a) A constitutional review is a sovereign, participatory process involving broad national dialogue, parliamentary debate and often referenda.
(b) The Commissions of Inquiries Act frames the exercise as a technical or administrative investigation, limiting its democratic legitimacy.
(c) The Act allows the President alone to establish Commissions, bypassing Parliament's central role in constitutional amendment.
(d) The concentration of power in the President undermined checks and balances.
(e) The recommendations of the Commission are not binding, could be ignored, or selectively adopted, weakening public trust in the process.

The Dibotelo Commission marked Botswana's first attempt at constitutional review since independence, but its reliance on the Commission of Inquiries Act gravely undermined its legitimacy.

The Dibotelo Commission episode is instructive. It reveals what happens when constitutional review is approached through the wrong legal framework. The Commissions of Inquiry Act was designed for a different purpose-to investigate specific problems and report findings. It assumes a technical, fact-finding exercise, not a participatory, sovereignty-expressing process. It concentrates power in the President, bypassing Parliament and the people. It produces recommendations that are not binding, that can be ignored or selectively adopted.

This is not how constitutional review should be conducted. A genuine review process must be sovereign, not subordinate. It must be participatory, not technocratic. It must involve Parliament and the people, not just the Executive. It must produce outcomes that are binding, not merely advisory. The Dibotelo Commission, whatever its intentions, could not meet these standards because it was operating under the wrong legal framework.

The historical realities discussed above make the process especially important in any contemporary constitutional review. The legitimacy deficit of the founding moment and the subsequent attempt by the Dibotelo Commission cannot be corrected solely by inserting progressive clauses; it must be addressed through comprehensive constitutional review and a participatory and inclusive process.

The lesson is clear: you cannot fix a process deficit with content fixes. Inserting progressive clauses into a Constitution that lacks popular ownership does not create legitimacy. The people may appreciate the new rights on paper, but they will not feel that the Constitution is theirs. True legitimacy requires that the people be involved in shaping the Constitution, that their voices be heard and their contributions reflected. This is what a participatory process can achieve and why it is essential for Botswana's constitutional review.

7.3 WHY PROCESS MATTERS AS MUCH AS CONTENT

7.3.1 The Legitimacy Argument

Legitimacy refers to the belief that a constitution deserves obedience. Scholars identify three forms:

- Legal legitimacy (proper procedures followed)
- Sociological legitimacy (public acceptance)
- Moral legitimacy (perceived fairness)

A constitution produced through an inclusive, transparent and participatory process is more likely to enjoy all three.

I have often argued that constitutional authority is weakened when people experience the constitution as something "done to them" rather than "created by them." The tagline often used by civil society: "nothing for us, without us," applies with equal force when it comes to constitutional review exercise.

Legal legitimacy is about following the rules. If a constitution is adopted through procedures that are themselves constitutionally prescribed, it has legal legitimacy. But legal legitimacy alone is thin. A constitution could be legally adopted, yet lack public acceptance or moral authority.

Sociological legitimacy is about public acceptance. Do the people actually believe the constitution deserves obedience? Do they comply with its provisions not just from fear of punishment, but from a sense of obligation? Sociological legitimacy is earned through process. When people participate in creating a constitution, they are more likely to accept its authority.

Moral legitimacy is about perceived fairness. Does the constitution treat all citizens with equal concern and respect? Does it protect fundamental rights? Does it create institutions that are likely to govern justly? Moral legitimacy depends partly on content—the actual provisions of the constitution—but also on process. A constitution produced through an inclusive process is more likely to be perceived as fair, even by those who disagree with some of its provisions.

The civil society slogan, "nothing for us, without us," captures the essence of the legitimacy argument. People resist being acted upon. They want to be participants in decisions that affect their lives. This is true of legislation, of policy, and supremely of constitutions. A constitution that is made without the people cannot claim their allegiance.

7.3.2 Process and Constitutional Endurance

Comparative research shows that constitutions developed through participatory processes tend to:

- Last longer
- Be amended less frequently
- Be defended by citizens during political crises

This is because people are more willing to protect what they helped build.

The link between process and endurance is intuitive but also empirically supported. When people have invested time and energy in creating a constitution, when they have debated its provisions and contributed their views, they develop a stake in its survival. They are more likely to resist attempts to subvert it, more likely to defend it against authoritarian encroachment, more likely to pass on its values to the next generation.

Conversely, constitutions imposed by elites or external powers are fragile. When crises come, when political actors are tempted to overreach, there is no popular constituency to defend the constitutional order. The constitution exists on paper, but not in the hearts of the people. It can be set aside with little resistance.

This is why the process is not merely a matter of democratic principle, but of practical consequence. A participatory process is an investment in constitutional endurance. The time and resources spent on consultation, deliberation, and consensus-building pay dividends in the form of a constitution that can withstand the tests of time and trouble.

7.4 CONVERSATIONAL CONSTITUTIONALISM EXPLAINED

7.4.1 What Is Conversational Constitutionalism?

Conversational constitutionalism is the idea that constitution-making should be a sustained national conversation, not a one-off consultation. It emphasises:

- Dialogue over decree
- Listening over persuasion
- Mutual learning between citizens and experts.

Rather than viewing citizens as passive recipients of expert knowledge, conversational constitutionalism treats them as co-authors of constitutional meaning.

The concept of conversational constitutionalism offers a distinctive approach to constitutional review. It rejects the model in which experts draft a constitution and then present it to the public for ratification, with, at most, a token consultation along the way. Instead, it envisions a process in which citizens and experts engage in ongoing dialogue, each learning from the other.

In this model, citizens are not passive recipients of expert knowledge. They are active participants in shaping constitutional meaning. Their lived experiences, their values, and their aspirations are essential inputs to the constitutional project. Experts bring technical knowledge about constitutional design, comparative experience and legal craft. But they do not have a monopoly on wisdom about how a society should be governed.

Dialogue replaces decree. Instead of being told what the constitution will contain, citizens are invited into a conversation about what it should contain. Listening replaces persuasion. Instead of experts trying to convince citizens to accept predetermined outcomes, experts listen to citizens' concerns and incorporate them into the drafting process. Mutual learning replaces one-way instruction. Both citizens and experts emerge from the process with a deeper understanding.

7.4.2 Theoretical Foundations

This concept draws from:

- Deliberative democracy theory
- African traditions of consultation and kgotla dialogue
- Participatory governance models promoted by IDEA

In the Botswana context, conversational constitutionalism resonates strongly with indigenous practices of collective decision-making, *therisanyo* (consultation), even though modern political systems have often sidelined these traditions.

Conversational constitutionalism is not an imported idea. It resonates deeply with Botswana's own traditions. The kgotla system, in which community members gather to discuss matters of common concern and reach decisions through dialogue, embodies the same values that conversational constitutionalism seeks to promote. *Therisanyo* (consultation) is a deeply rooted cultural practice.

The challenge is to translate these traditions from the local to the national level. A kgotla works for a village community; a constitutional convention must work for an entire nation. But the principles are the same: inclusive dialogue, respectful listening, collective decision-making. Modern technologies and methods can extend these principles to a national scale, enabling millions of citizens to participate in the constitutional conversation.

Deliberative democracy theory provides additional resources. It emphasises that democratic legitimacy requires not just aggregation of preferences through voting, but genuine deliberation among citizens. Through deliberation, preferences can be transformed, mutual understanding can be deepened, and consensus can emerge. Constitutional review offers an opportunity for national deliberation on a grand scale.

7.5 PROCESS AS CIVIC EDUCATION

7.5.1 Learning Through Participation

One of the most powerful outcomes of a well-designed constitutional process is constitutional literacy. Participation teaches citizens:

- How power is structured
- What rights mean in practice
- How institutions should be held accountable

Constitutional review literature shows that constitution-making processes often function as the largest civic education exercise a country will ever undertake.

The educational dimension of constitutional review is often overlooked but immensely valuable. When citizens participate in constitutional processes, they learn about their constitution. They learn how government is structured, what rights they have, and how institutions are supposed to work. This learning is not abstract; it is connected to a concrete process in which their participation matters.

Consider what citizens learn through participation. They learn about the separation of powers as they consider whether to strengthen the legislature or limit the executive. They learn about federalism as they debate the allocation of powers between national and local governments. They learn about rights as they advocate for protections that matter to them. This learning is deeper and more lasting than anything that could be conveyed through textbooks or lectures.

Constitution-making is often the largest civic education exercise a country will ever undertake. It reaches millions of citizens through consultations, media coverage, civic education campaigns, and public debate. It creates a national conversation about fundamental values and institutional design. It leaves in its wake a citizenry that is more knowledgeable about and more engaged with their constitution.

7.5.2 From Subjects to Citizens

Where people participate meaningfully, they begin to see themselves not as subjects of authority, but as constitutional citizens. This shift is essential for democratic consolidation.

The transformation from subject to citizen is profound. Subjects obey because they must. They are passive recipients of decisions made by others. They may comply with the law, but they do not identify with it. They do not see themselves as part of the political community that makes the law.

Citizens, by contrast, obey because they have consented. They see themselves as authors of the laws that bind them. They participate in political life, hold their government accountable, and defend their rights. They identify with the political community and take responsibility for its fate.

Constitutional review can catalyse this transformation. When people participate in shaping their constitution, they experience themselves as citizens. They see that their voice matters, that their contribution can make a difference. This experience can spill over into other areas of political life, creating a more engaged and empowered citizenry.

7.6 RISKS OF A POOR PROCESS

7.6.1 Elite Capture

When constitutional review is dominated by political elites, lawyers, or consultants, it risks becoming disconnected from public needs. Elite capture often leads to:

- Technocratic language
- Limited public ownership
- Suspicion and resistance

Elite capture is the most common risk in constitutional review. Those who hold power naturally seek to retain it. Those with expertise naturally believe they know best. The result can be a process that is dominated by a small group, that uses language ordinary people cannot understand, that produces a document reflecting elite interests rather than public needs.

The consequences of elite capture are predictable. The constitution lacks public ownership. Citizens do not see themselves in it. They may comply with it from fear, but they will not defend it. When political crises come, there is no popular constituency for constitutionalism. The elite who crafted the constitution may try to defend it, but they lack the numbers to prevail against determined opponents.

Suspicion and resistance are natural responses to elite capture. Citizens who feel excluded from the process are likely to suspect that the resulting constitution serves interests other than their own. They may resist its implementation, challenge its legitimacy, or simply ignore its provisions. A constitution that cannot command voluntary compliance is a failure.

7.6.2 Token Participation

Public participation that is rushed, poorly advertised, or ignored creates frustration and cynicism. Governments must avoid tokenism when engaged in the process of constitutional review. Tokenism is worse than no participation because it erodes trust.

Token participation is participation in name only. Citizens are invited to consultations, but their views are not taken seriously. Submissions are collected, but not analysed. Feedback is promised, but not provided. The process creates the appearance of participation without the substance.

Tokenism is worse than no participation at all. No participation at least sets expectations low. Citizens know they are not involved and adjust their expectations accordingly. Tokenism raises expectations (citizens are told their voice matters) and then disappoints them. The result is not just cynicism about the constitutional process, but cynicism about the entire political system.

Governments must avoid tokenism at all costs. If participation is to be offered, it must be genuine. That means adequate time for consultation, proper advertising to reach all affected communities, serious analysis of submissions, and transparent feedback about how public input influenced the final product. Anything less is worse than nothing.

7.7 BOTSWANA-SPECIFIC IMPLICATIONS

For Botswana, the constitutional review process must:

- Rebuild the legitimacy lost at independence
- Reflect social diversity (youth, women, minorities, rural communities)
- Align democratic ideals with lived experience

I often emphasise that constitutional reform should be transformative, not merely corrective, and transformation begins with process.

Botswana faces a distinctive set of challenges and opportunities in its constitutional review. The legitimacy deficit from the founding moment must be addressed. This cannot be done by simply inserting progressive clauses into the existing document. It requires a process that involves the people, which gives them ownership of the resulting constitution.

Social diversity must be reflected. Botswana is not homogeneous. It includes youth and elders, women and men, minorities and majorities, and urban and rural communities. A constitution that speaks only to some of these groups will not command the allegiance of all. The process must be designed to reach every community, to hear every voice, and to ensure that the final document reflects the diversity of the nation.

Democratic ideals must be aligned with lived experience. It is not enough to proclaim rights on paper; those rights must be real in people's lives. The constitutional process must attend to the gap between constitutional promise and social reality. It must ask not only what rights should be protected, but also what obstacles prevent people from enjoying those rights and how those obstacles can be overcome.

Constitutional reform should be transformative, not merely corrective. Correction fixes what is broken; transformation creates something new. Botswana has an opportunity not just to patch the 1966 Constitution, but to create a constitution for the twenty-first century, one that reflects the values and aspirations of today's Batswana. Transformation begins with the process. A transformative process can produce a transformative document.

7.8 CONCLUSION: PROCESS AS CONSTITUTIONAL SUBSTANCE

This chapter has shown that the constitutional process is not merely a pathway to a document; it is part of the constitution itself. Participation, dialogue, and inclusion shape how the constitution will be interpreted, defended, and lived.

For constitutional literacy purposes, learners must understand that:

- A good constitution can fail if born badly
- A participatory process educates, empowers, and legitimises
- Conversational constitutionalism offers Botswana a culturally resonant and democratically robust model

The central insight of this chapter is that process is not separate from substance; it is part of substance. How a constitution is made affects what it means, how it functions, and whether it endures. A constitution born through exclusion will bear the marks of its birth, however elegant its provisions. A constitution born through participation will carry the energy of its creation, however imperfect its drafting.

A good constitution can fail if born badly. The most beautifully drafted document will not command allegiance if the people had no hand in its making. Conversely, a constitution with flaws may succeed if the people feel ownership of it and are committed to working within its framework. Process matters that much.

A participatory process educates, empowers and legitimises. It teaches citizens about their constitution, giving them a stake in its success. It creates the conditions for voluntary compliance and active defence. These outcomes are as important as any provision in the document.

Conversational constitutionalism offers Botswana a model that resonates with its own traditions. The kgotla, *therisanyo*, and other practices of consultation and dialogue provide cultural resources for designing a participatory process. By drawing on these traditions while also learning from comparative experience, Botswana can create a constitutional review process that is both democratically robust and culturally resonant.

The chapters that follow provide the detailed roadmap for such a process. They address the preliminary questions that must be answered before the review begins. They examine the roles of civil society, political parties, and media. They articulate guiding principles. They trace the phases of review from preparation through adoption. Throughout, they are informed by the conviction that process matters, that how Botswana reviews its constitution will shape not only the final document, but the future of its democracy.

RECAP AND TRANSITION

Recap: This introductory chapter to Part 2 has established the fundamental argument that process is as important as content in constitutional review. It has examined the legitimacy argument, showing that constitutions born through participation enjoy legal, sociological, and moral legitimacy. It has explored the historical context of Botswana's 1966 Constitution and the Dibotelo Commission, revealing the legitimacy deficit that a comprehensive review must address. It has introduced the concept of conversational constitutionalism, emphasising dialogue, listening, and mutual learning. It has explained how the process serves as civic education, transforming subjects into citizens. It has warned against the risks of elite capture and token participation. And it has drawn out the specific implications for Botswana, arguing that reform should be transformative, not merely corrective.

Transition: Having established why process matters, the next chapter turns to the foundational questions that must be answered before any constitutional review process can begin. Chapter Nine addresses the preliminary questions: Do we need a comprehensive review or an incremental amendment? Who should frame the roadmap? Is a stakeholder conference required? Who should draft the terms of reference? What is a constitutional assembly, and how should it be composed? These questions are not merely technical; they go to the heart of legitimacy and must be answered through inclusive dialogue and careful deliberation.

CHAPTER EIGHT

PRELIMINARY QUESTIONS – CONSTITUTIONAL REVIEW PROCESS

8.1 INTRODUCTION

Before outlining the stages of a constitutional review process, it is important to reflect on key preliminary questions that arise whenever a country considers making a new constitution or fundamentally revising an existing one. These questions are not exhaustive, but they go to the heart of legitimacy, durability, and public trust. Comparative experience shows that the way a constitution is made is often as important as its final content. Poorly designed processes risk elite capture, exclusion, and long-term instability, while inclusive and transparent processes can contribute to peacebuilding, national ownership, and democratic consolidation.

The decision to embark on constitutional review is momentous. It signals that the existing constitutional framework is, in some significant respect, inadequate; that it no longer serves the people as it should, that it fails to reflect their values, that it cannot address the challenges they face. But the decision to review is only the beginning. Many more decisions follow, each shaping the process and its outcome.

This chapter addresses the questions that must be answered at the very start of any constitutional review process. These questions are preliminary in the sense that they come before the detailed design of the process, but they are fundamental in the sense that they determine everything that follows. Getting the answers right is essential to legitimacy; getting them wrong can doom the entire enterprise.

The questions are interconnected. The answer to one affects the others. Who frames the roadmap influences what guidelines are developed.

Whether a stakeholder conference is held affects who drafts the terms of reference. The composition of a constitutional assembly shapes how inclusive the process will be. These interconnections mean that the preliminary questions must be considered together, as a package, rather than in isolation.

Comparative experience provides guidance, but not formulas. All countries' circumstances are different. What worked in South Africa may not work in Botswana. What failed in Kenya may succeed elsewhere. The task is not to copy but to learn: to extract principles and practices that can be adapted to local conditions.

8.2 DO WE NEED A COMPREHENSIVE CONSTITUTIONAL REVIEW?

Any nation that embarks on a constitutional review process must ask itself a series of fundamental questions before initiating the process. The starting point for constitution-making must address the most basic question: "Do you need a new constitution?" Failure to ask this basic question, as exemplified by the process in Afghanistan, can lead to unnecessary effort, suggesting that cleaning up an older constitution might have been sufficient. When a nation decides to embark on this journey, the initial design must prioritise inclusiveness, participation, and transparency to ensure the outcome has legitimacy and contributes to a durable peace.

The question, "Do we need a constitutional review?" is not as simple as it appears. It has multiple dimensions. Is the existing constitution fundamentally flawed, or does it merely require amendments? Are the problems with the constitution itself, or with how it has been implemented? Would a new constitution address the grievances that have prompted calls for change, or would it simply create new problems?

The Afghan experience is instructive. Following the fall of the Taliban, there was international pressure to adopt a new constitution. The process was rushed, dominated by elites and insufficiently attentive to local conditions. The resulting constitution, while technically adequate, failed to command broad allegiance and did not prevent the subsequent collapse of constitutional order. Some observers have suggested that a more modest process of amending the existing constitution might have been more appropriate, allowing for gradual reform rather than wholesale replacement.

This does not mean that a comprehensive review is never appropriate. South Africa's transition from apartheid to democracy required a completely new constitution; the old order was so thoroughly illegitimate that it could not be salvaged through amendment. Kenya's 2010 constitution represented a fundamental break with the past, addressing deep-seated problems of ethnic exclusion, executive dominance, and centralised power. In both cases, a comprehensive review was necessary.

The key is to ask the question honestly and to answer it through inclusive deliberation. The people who will live under the constitution should have a voice in determining whether a new one is needed. Their perceptions of the existing constitution's legitimacy, their aspirations for the future, their sense of what problems need solving—all should inform the decision.

When initiating constitutional change, the context often dictates the timing and urgency. In the Philippines, the process of drafting the 1987 Constitution was undertaken with great urgency by President Cory Aquino following the overthrow of Marcos, driven by a fear of a military coup. She believed that quickly establishing a new constitution would minimise the military's power and act as a deterrent. In contrast, South Africa's path began with intense, high-stakes negotiations between the old apartheid regime and representatives of the majority. This negotiation resulted in the 1993 interim constitution, which was itself passed through the procedures of the old constitution and set out the process for creating the final 1996 constitution. This sequencing, which carefully dealt with preliminary issues, ultimately facilitated the success of the constitution-making process.

Context matters enormously. In the Philippines, urgency was driven by fear of military intervention. The new constitution was seen as a bulwark against a return to authoritarianism. In South Africa, the process was necessarily gradual and negotiated, given the deep divisions and the need to secure agreement from both the outgoing regime and the liberation movements. Each context shaped the process in distinctive ways.

Botswana's context is different from both. There is no recent authoritarian regime to guard against, no violent conflict to resolve. The impetus for review comes from a different source: the gradual accumulation of social, economic, and political changes, the evolution of human rights norms, and the desire for deeper democratic participation. This context allows for a more deliberate process, one that can prioritise inclusivity and participation over speed.

Kenya provides an instructive example of a convoluted start and restart, demonstrating that early design choices have long-lasting political consequences. The first major constitutional review process (2000–2005) began following national conferences, which secured a consensus on both procedure and the agenda after years of pressure for reform. A Constitutional Review Commission was mandated to prepare a draft after collecting public views, holding at least one meeting in every parliamentary constituency. However, this inclusive process was ultimately killed when a court ruled that a referendum was necessary, giving the government, which resisted the proposed changes, the opportunity to alter the popular draft, which the people subsequently rejected in the 2005 referendum. After post-election violence in 2008, a new process was compelled by external pressure from the international community, restarting with a committee of local and foreign experts tasked with resolving contentious issues using existing drafts.

Kenya's experience illustrates the dangers of getting the preliminary questions wrong. The first process was inclusive and participatory, but a court decision and political manipulation derailed it. The second process was more elite-driven, imposed under international pressure. The contrast between the two and the eventual success of the 2010 constitution offer lessons about the importance of getting the process design right from the start.

From these diverse experiences, several best practices for starting a constitutional process emerge. Firstly, there is a critical need to explicitly agree on the need for reform and the modalities of the process. This initial agreement should define the guiding principles for both the process (e.g., transparency, inclusivity) and the document's content, sometimes taking the form of entrenched clauses about fundamental principles to be incorporated later. Secondly, constitution-making processes often face a dilemma regarding sequencing: whether to hold elections before the constitutional process, and whether to consult the public before or after a draft is prepared. Consulting the public *prior* to drafting provides greater scope for popular views and broadens the reform agenda beyond elite concerns, as seen in the Philippines, Fiji, Kenya, and Uganda. Thirdly, time is paramount; rushing the process, especially in post-conflict environments, can lead to the exclusion of key actors, undermine legitimacy, and result in a lack of trust. Inclusive processes like those in Uganda, South Africa, and Kenya have taken years to complete because of special measures adopted for greater public participation, inclusion, and the promotion of national ownership.

These best practices guide Botswana. First, there must be explicit agreement on the need for reform and the modalities of the process. This agreement should not be assumed; it should be deliberately sought through inclusive dialogue. Second, the sequencing question must be addressed. Public consultation before drafting is generally preferable, as it allows popular views to shape the agenda rather than merely reacting to an elite-produced draft. Third, adequate time must be allocated. Rushing the process would be a grave mistake, undermining the very legitimacy that the review seeks to achieve.

Ultimately, the optimal way to start the process is to establish a well-designed road map that prioritises democratic principles over speed. A preliminary step should guide this plan: the national leadership having the political will to genuinely promote the broadest possible participation and consensus. This political commitment must translate into allocating sufficient resources and time, managing public expectations, and defining the agenda for reform to ensure the "journey" is respected as much as the final "destination." Just as an architect needs to lay a sturdy and widely agreed-upon foundation before raising a structure, constitution-makers must establish a legitimate, inclusive process to ensure the resultant constitution can bear the weight of a nation's future.

The metaphor of architecture is apt. A building is only as strong as its foundation. A constitution is only as legitimate as the process that produces it. Investing in the foundation (in getting the preliminary questions right, in building consensus, in designing an inclusive process) is essential to the long-term success of the constitutional project.

8.3 HOW DOES POLITICS INTERFERE WITH OR DIRECT CONSTITUTION-MAKING OR REVISION?

The initiation of a process to make a new constitution or fundamentally revise an old one is a crucial moment that sets the tone for the entire constitutional project. This starting phase must begin with a fundamental consensus on the need for reform and a conscious commitment to a transparent, inclusive, and nationally owned design. Historically, constitution-making has often been an act of power consolidation, crafted behind closed doors by new rulers or imperial powers. Still, contemporary best practice emphasises designing a participatory roadmap that maximises peacebuilding opportunities and builds trust among deeply divided factions. The key initial tasks involve deciding if a new process is even necessary, agreeing upon the reform agenda, and establishing the legal and political framework for the "journey" ahead.

The relationship between law and politics in constitution-making is complex and sometimes tense. Law provides the framework—the procedures, the institutions, the limits. Politics provides the driving force—the interests, the conflicts, the compromises. Both are essential, but they can also work at cross-purposes.

The earliest stages of the process are fundamentally directed and interfered with by the complex interplay of existing law and high-stakes politics. If a country has an existing constitution, the legal starting point should address the process of amendment or replacement. Legal continuity is often sought by making constitutional changes through the procedures of the existing law, as South Africa did when its interim constitution was passed pursuant to the procedures outlined in the apartheid constitution to provide a solid legal foundation for the permanent document. However, the scope of reform is intensely political: constitution-makers must decide whether to pursue incremental change, which risks resistance from existing regimes, or a complete replacement (a *de novo* constitution), which can escalate political stakes and societal divisions.

South Africa's approach was masterful. By using the procedures of the apartheid constitution to adopt the interim constitution, they maintained legal continuity while enabling fundamental change. The interim constitution was legally valid under the old order, but it created the framework for a new order. This approach minimised legal challenges and provided a stable foundation for the transition.

The choice between incremental amendment and wholesale replacement is profoundly political. Incremental amendment may be less disruptive, but it may also be insufficient to address deep-seated problems. It may leave in place structures and assumptions that perpetuate injustice. Complete replacement offers the opportunity for fundamental transformation, but it also raises the stakes and can intensify political conflict. There is no right answer that applies in all contexts; the choice must be made based on the specific circumstances of each country.

Politics frequently interferes with or directs the start of the process by imposing pressure or generating a crisis. The impetus for change often comes from political action by civil society or "informal" networks, sometimes against the resistance of those already in power who achieved their position under the existing constitution. In situations of conflict or transition, the process may be compelled by external pressure from the international community or by internal negotiations between warring groups. This political reality means processes are often negotiated rather than rationally designed; the details of the process may be debated fiercely, such as the makeup of a constitutional commission or its terms of reference. The greatest pressure point is establishing the timetable, as international actors often impose short timetables that risk undermining the possibility of a genuinely participatory and nationally owned process.

The tension between rational design and political negotiation is inherent in constitution-making. Ideally, the process would be designed by neutral experts based on best practices and tailored to local conditions. In reality, the process is shaped by power: by who has it, who wants it, who is resisting whom. This is not necessarily a bad thing. Politics is the means through which societies make collective decisions. But it does mean that the process design must be attentive to political dynamics and must build in safeguards against domination by the most powerful actors.

The timetable is often the most contested issue. International actors, concerned about stability and eager to show progress, may push for rapid completion. Domestic actors, who benefit from the status quo, may seek to delay. Those seeking change may want enough time to mobilise and participate, but not so much that momentum is lost. Balancing these pressures is difficult, but the weight of comparative experience suggests that erring on the side of more time is safer. Rushed processes produce shallow legitimacy.

Moreover, the political class, consisting of elected officials and political parties, inevitably dominates decision-making about the process structure, creating a constant tension between the people and the politicians. Politicians, often viewed with cynicism for serving narrow, partisan interests, seek to control the process because of the high stakes involved. This political dominance means that the initial design must guard against elite capture, where consultation is manipulated or used as a mere formality to confer spurious legitimacy. The starting design attempts to mitigate this risk by emphasising early and extensive public participation (such as prior consultation before a draft is prepared), which broadens the reform agenda and serves as a crucial check on unilateral elite action.

The dominance of politicians in constitution-making is a double-edged sword. On one hand, politicians are elected representatives who can claim a mandate to speak for the people. On the other hand, they have interests of their own—in retaining power, in advancing partisan agendas, and in protecting their positions. These interests may not align with the broader public interest.

The solution is not to exclude politicians (that would be both impossible and undemocratic), but to build in countervailing forces. Early and extensive public participation can broaden the agenda and create a public constituency for reform that politicians cannot ignore. Civil society can monitor the process and advocate for inclusive outcomes. The media can inform the public and expose manipulation. These checks on elite power are essential to preventing capture.

In essence, the beginning of a constitutional project is a delicate balance of law and political necessity. While legal frameworks must be considered for validity, politics determines feasibility. The best practice for starting involves national leaders demonstrating the necessary political will to commit adequate resources and time to an inclusive roadmap. By agreeing on guiding principles for both the process (like transparency and inclusion) and the content, a foundation is laid that is resistant to being derailed by political actors or legalistic challenges, ultimately building the necessary trust for a durable constitutional order.

The key insight is that law and politics must work together. Law provides the framework, but politics provides the will. A legally perfect process that lacks political support will fail. A politically popular process that ignores legal requirements may produce a constitution that is vulnerable to challenge. The art of constitutional design lies in integrating the two: creating a process that is both legally sound and politically sustainable.

8.4 WHO SHOULD FRAME THE ROADMAP OF THE CONSTITUTION-MAKING OR REVISION PROCESS?

The creation or fundamental revision of a national constitution is not simply a technical, legal endeavour, but a highly political process that dictates the future framework of governance and societal relations. Therefore, the way the process begins, the initial choices made about its design, is paramount to ensuring the constitution's legitimacy, durability, and success in securing a durable peace, especially in war-torn or deeply divided countries. The process must commence with the fundamental task of addressing the constitutional starting point, determining if a new constitution is truly needed, or if a more modest revision would suffice. If major reform is deemed necessary, the initial stages must focus on building consensus and establishing a transparent, inclusive roadmap for the entire constitutional journey.

The roadmap is the plan that guides the entire constitutional process. It sets out the sequence of steps, the institutions to be created, the timelines to be followed, the methods of participation, and the mechanisms for adoption. Getting the roadmap right is essential to legitimacy; getting it wrong can doom the process from the start.

The roadmap, or design, is the strategic plan that dictates the sequence, institutions, objectives and deadlines leading to the constitution's adoption. It provides guidance on procedure and timing, informs the public of the process, and minimises disputes among actors. The creation of this roadmap is an intensely political and negotiated process where several factors come into interplay.

The roadmap is not a technical document to be produced by experts in isolation. It is a political document that reflects choices about who will be involved, how decisions will be made, and what values will guide the process. Its creation must itself be inclusive and participatory.

The political parties and national government are usually central to determining the course. The roadmap is often found in an agreement among key political actors, an ordinary law, or as part of an interim constitution. Where a constituent assembly or constitutional commission is established, the legal framework that sets up these institutions often defines aspects of the agenda and sequence. In conflict or post-conflict settings, the parties to the peace process frequently dictate the roadmap, often through a peace agreement, which then determines the legal and political arrangements for the new constitutional order. Leaders of the warring factions often dominate this stage. Where a constituent assembly or constitutional commission is in charge of the process, it may prepare its own roadmap or strategic plan. Civil society and political parties frequently have input, and sometimes the international community influences the design, particularly in situations of intense internal conflict. However, while civil society can promote change, it typically does not possess the power to make a legally binding roadmap.

The question of who frames the roadmap is thus a question of power. Those who control the roadmap control the process. This is why the initial stages are often contested: different actors seek to shape the roadmap to serve their interests.

In Botswana's context, the answer to this question must be guided by the principles of inclusivity and participation. The roadmap should not be framed by the executive alone, as occurred with the Dibotelo Commission. Nor should it be framed exclusively by political parties, however representative they may be. Instead, the framing of the roadmap should involve a broad range of stakeholders: government, Parliament, political parties, civil society, traditional leaders, women's organisations, youth groups and others. Their involvement at this early stage builds ownership and ensures that the roadmap reflects a genuine national consensus.

The complexity and high stakes of constitution-making mean that the design process is not "rationally designed," but is usually negotiated, often requiring hard bargaining among key actors.

Acknowledging that the process is negotiated rather than designed is important. It means that perfection is not the goal. The goal is a workable compromise that enough key actors can accept. This does not mean abandoning principles; it means recognising that principles must be applied in contexts of power, interest and conflict.

8.5 IS A STAKEHOLDER CONFERENCE AT THE BEGINNING REQUIRED, AND IF SO, WHO SHOULD ATTEND AND WHAT SHOULD BE THE AGENDA?

There is "no single correct way of designing a constitution-making process." Preliminary discussions, often referred to as a roundtable or national conference, are essential tools for consensus-building at the initial stage, particularly in transitional or conflict-ridden societies. A large-scale, inclusive conference or roundtable is crucial for several reasons:

1. **Establishing Consensus.** The first step in any constitution-making process is to agree on the need for reform, the principles underlying it, and the modalities of the process. A roundtable can serve as an informal consultative process to negotiate initial steps and secure agreements among key actors, which is particularly important when mistrust runs deep.
2. **Preventing Exclusion and Conflict.** Exclusion or marginalisation of key actors breeds resentment and can sow the seeds for renewed violence. Inclusive processes, such as conferences, aim to draw in all key stakeholders to foster a sense of responsibility and ensure peace is less likely to collapse.

3. **Developing Guiding Principles.** Conferences are vital for negotiating the guiding principles for both the process (e.g. transparency and participation) and the content of the future constitution. These principles provide a shared vision of a better future and assure minority groups that their interests will be protected, encouraging them to join the process rather than undermine it.

A stakeholder conference is not merely a nice-to-have; it is essential to legitimacy. It provides a forum in which key actors can come together, express their views, negotiate differences, and build consensus. It signals that the process is open and inclusive, that all voices matter. It creates relationships and understandings that can sustain the process through the inevitable conflicts that arise.

Preliminary meetings should strive to be as inclusive as possible. While participants will vary by context, they typically include political stakeholders (e.g., government representatives, political parties, including opposition groups, and leaders of warring factions), civil society, marginalised groups, and experts and external actors.

Inclusivity means more than inviting a few token representatives from different sectors. It means actively reaching out to groups that have historically been excluded: women, youth, ethnic minorities, rural communities, and persons with disabilities. It means providing the resources and support they need to participate effectively. It means designing the conference in ways that enable genuine participation, not just passive attendance.

The agenda of a preliminary conference focuses on securing foundational agreements related to the *process* and defining the *content* boundaries. Key items typically include:

- **Process and Modalities:** Establishing the roadmap or timetable for the entire constitutional effort. This involves deciding on the institutions to be used (e.g. commissions, assemblies) and procedures for their selection.

- **Guiding Principles:** Establishing the core principles that will govern the constitution's content, such as human rights, social justice, and federalism. These principles act as preconditions or assurances for parties who fear being excluded or disadvantaged by a majority vote.
- **Identifying Constitutional Issues:** Identifying the constitutional issues that must be addressed, allowing the reform agenda to be decided consultatively and broadening it beyond the narrow interests of political elites.

The agenda should focus on what needs to be agreed upon before the detailed process begins. Process and modalities come first: how will the review be conducted, who will be involved, and what timeline will be followed. Guiding principles come next: what values will inform the new constitution, what basic commitments must it respect. Identification of constitutional issues follows: what topics must be addressed and what problems must be solved?

In essence, the initial stakeholder conference is where a country transforms a political crisis into a defined project, setting the stage for either a collaborative, people-driven process that maximises peacebuilding or a constrained, elite-controlled exercise vulnerable to failure.

The stakeholder conference is thus a critical juncture. Done well, it can launch a process that builds consensus, includes all voices, and produces a constitution with broad ownership. Done poorly, it can entrench divisions, exclude key actors, and set the stage for failure. Getting it right requires careful planning, genuine commitment to inclusivity and skilled facilitation.

8.6 WHO SHOULD DRAFT THE TERMS OF REFERENCE? THE EXECUTIVE, THE STAKEHOLDER CONFERENCE, THE CONSTITUTIONAL ASSEMBLY?

The initiation of a process to create a new constitution or fundamentally revise an existing one is perhaps the most critical stage, setting the ultimate trajectory for the nation's political and social future. This undertaking should begin with a conscious recognition that constitution-making is inherently a deeply political and sensitive process, not merely a technical legal exercise. The first logical task is determining whether a new constitution is truly needed at all, or if a more modest reform might suffice. Once the necessity for major change is established, the start must prioritise three core principles: inclusiveness, participation, and transparency, to maximise peacebuilding opportunities and foster the trust essential for a durable document.

The terms of reference define the mandate of the constitutional review body. They specify what it is supposed to do, what issues it must address, what principles it must follow, and what timeline it must observe. Getting the terms of reference right is essential; vague or contested terms of reference can lead to confusion, conflict, and paralysis.

Framing the roadmap and terms of reference. The foundational document that outlines the process, sometimes referred to as the "design," "blueprint" or "roadmap," sets forth the sequence, deadlines, institutions, and objectives leading to the constitution's adoption. The determination of who should frame the terms of reference is typically a complex legal and political negotiation, often dominated by those who hold power or who are party to a peace agreement.

In many contexts, the government makes the initial decision, sometimes after discussions with relevant groups. The government or head of state may use an executive order or general constitutional power to set up a constitutional commission or other body. However, pressure from within the government is sometimes self-interested rather than focused on the national interest, which necessitates checks on this power. The legislature frequently sets up the process by passing ordinary laws or through entrenched legislation. The law or other legal document establishing a process often defines some of the key constitutional issues to be considered, acting as the document's terms of reference. In post-conflict or deeply divided situations, the roadmap and terms of reference are often hammered out through intense negotiations among the parties to the peace process or in roundtables. These negotiations result in agreements that define the process, the areas of reform, and the fundamental principles to be incorporated. The South African interim constitution, for example, was the product of such negotiations among the main political parties and set out the process for the final constitution. While a Constitutional Assembly (CA) or Commission may be mandated to prepare its own roadmap, the CA usually comes into existence *after* the roadmap has been set out by law or political agreement. Examples like the 1972 terms of reference for Papua New Guinea's Constitutional Planning Committee illustrate the legislature setting the issues to be considered.

The lesson from comparative experience is that the terms of reference should be drafted through an inclusive process that involves all key stakeholders. Exclusive drafting by the executive risks capture and manipulation. Exclusive drafting by the legislature may reflect partisan interests rather than national consensus. The ideal is a process in which government, Parliament, political parties, civil society, and other stakeholders come together to negotiate and agree on the terms of reference. This may occur through a stakeholder conference, through parliamentary hearings, or through a specially constituted drafting committee.

8.7 WHAT IS A CONSTITUTIONAL ASSEMBLY AND HOW SHOULD IT BE COMPOSED?

A Constitutional Assembly (CA) is a body designed to represent the nation, assigned the task of debating in detail a draft constitution and approving that draft. The term "constituent assembly" often implies a body solely or mainly vested with "constituent power", the primordial power of the people to constitute a frame of government. CAs differ from ordinary legislatures because they usually do not make ordinary laws, are focused on the constitution-making power of the people, and often involve greater public participation.

The concept of a constitutional assembly is rooted in the idea of constituent power—the power of the people to create or replace their constitution. This power is distinct from the ordinary powers of government. It is the power that creates the framework within which ordinary government operates. A constitutional assembly is the institutional embodiment of this constituent power.

The composition of constitutional assemblies varies widely in size and composition, but their design attempts to balance political expediency, technical competence, and broad representation. Assemblies are often formed through combinations of methods:

1. **Direct Election.** Members are directly elected, though this may still be subject to political party dominance. Bolivia's 2009 Constituent Assembly members were directly elected, though with complex rules designed around geographical and party representation.
2. **Representation by Existing Bodies.** Members are drawn from existing governmental bodies, such as the legislature (e.g., India's 1950 Constituent Assembly members were indirectly elected by provincial assemblies).
3. **Selection of Special Interest Groups.** To ensure broad representation and prevent traditional politicians from dominating, seats are sometimes reserved for marginalised groups like women, indigenous peoples, youth, and civil society representatives. Nepal's Constituent Assembly (an ongoing process) used a complex mixed system including single-member constituencies and party lists to ensure broad representation.

Each method has advantages and disadvantages. Direct election gives the assembly democratic legitimacy but may reproduce existing political dynamics. Representation through existing bodies is efficient but may entrench elite power. Reserved seats for marginalised groups ensure inclusion but may be seen as undemocratic if not accompanied by broader electoral legitimacy.

Constitution-makers face a dilemma in constructing the membership, needing to balance the wishes of the people with the necessity of having politicians and experts involved. India's process involved a complex arrangement of committees, including a small expert committee on financial matters composed of non-members of the assembly, alongside its large representative committees.

The Indian experience offers a model: a large, representative assembly for broad debate and decision, supplemented by smaller expert committees for detailed drafting on specialised topics. This combination of representation and expertise can produce a constitution that is both democratically legitimate and technically sound.

A successful constitutional start requires political leaders to manage the tension between quick action, driven by the urgency of conflict or crisis, and the necessity of allowing adequate time for inclusive and deliberative processes to build the national consensus required for long-term legitimacy.

The tension between speed and deliberation is real and must be managed. In some contexts, urgency is genuine: a peace agreement may be fragile, a transition may be precarious. But even in such contexts, cutting corners on participation and inclusion can undermine the very stability the process seeks to achieve. The challenge is to find the right balance, to move quickly enough to maintain momentum, but deliberately enough to build legitimacy.

8.8 WHAT GUIDELINES SHOULD BE DEVELOPED TO GUIDE THE PROCESS?

The process of making a new constitution or fundamentally revising an old one is a defining national moment that should begin with the creation of a clear, guiding framework. Since the manner in which a constitution is made is as important as the resulting content, especially in war-torn or divided countries, the first step is to establish an inclusive process designed to build a durable consensus and a foundation for democratic values. This necessity stems from the fact that conflicts often arise from disputes over rights, resources, identity, and power, and mistrust runs deep, making every point of tension potentially explosive. Therefore, rather than focusing solely on achieving a quick result, the focus must be on the "how" rather than the "what," ensuring that the process itself is designed to resolve conflict and establish a just social order.

Guidelines are the principles that govern the process. They are not detailed rules, but framework commitments that shape how decisions are made, who is involved, and what values are respected. Developing guidelines at the outset assures all participants that the process will be fair.

A successful initiation is marked by the development and commitment to a comprehensive set of guiding principles intended to govern the entire constitutional process. These principles serve as the terms of reference, providing assurance to minority groups and offering a shared vision of a better future. The sources identify several core principles that should be developed and adhered to from the outset, reflecting both historical context and broader international norms. The most critical among these are national ownership, inclusiveness, participation, and transparency.

National ownership means that the process is driven by local actors, not imposed from outside. International assistance may be valuable, but it must support, rather than supplant, local leadership. The constitution must be seen as the product of the nation's own deliberations, not as an import.

Inclusiveness means that all segments of society have the opportunity to participate. This includes not only political parties and organised interests, but also marginalised groups (women, youth, ethnic minorities, rural communities, persons with disabilities). Inclusiveness requires proactive outreach, not just open doors.

Participation means that involvement is meaningful, not merely symbolic. Participants must have genuine opportunities to influence outcomes. Their views must be heard, considered, and reflected in the final document. Token participation, as discussed earlier, is worse than none.

Transparency means that the process is open to public scrutiny. Meetings are public, documents are accessible, and decisions are explained. Transparency builds trust by demonstrating that nothing is hidden, that decisions are made on the merits rather than through backroom deals.

National ownership must be established immediately, meaning local actors determine the priorities and lead the process, because a constitution, like peace, cannot be imposed from outside. For the constitution to be credible and durable, its design must ensure that the voices of people from across society are heard and incorporated in its creation, fulfilling the requirements of inclusiveness and participation. This requires a proactive commitment to reaching marginalised segments of society, such as women, youth, indigenous populations, and the disabled, and ensuring that special measures are adopted for greater public participation throughout every stage.

Furthermore, transparency and accountability are essential guiding principles for the process. Transparency involves conducting the process in an open manner so that people are aware of what is happening and why, and confident that their voices are heard. This principle is not only a means of achieving integrity and legitimacy, but is a goal in itself, helping to minimise disputes and protect the integrity of the process. Finally, the guidelines must address the practical dimension, ensuring that sufficient time and resources are allocated to the process. Given the complexities of fostering dialogue and building trust in divided societies, inclusive processes inherently take considerable time, and the impulse to impose tight, short timetables must be resisted.

Time and resources are not afterthoughts; they are essential to legitimacy. An inclusive process cannot be rushed. It takes time to reach all communities, to translate materials, to hold consultations, to analyse submissions, to build consensus. It takes resources to pay for venues, facilitators, transportation, and media campaigns. Under-resourcing the process is a recipe for failure.

By adhering to these principles: national ownership, inclusivity, participation, transparency, and adequate resourcing, the beginning of the constitutional process transforms from a mere legal step into a strategic peacebuilding opportunity. When followed, these guidelines foster a sense of public ownership of the constitution, which increases its legitimacy and the likelihood that citizens will protect it and exercise their duties under the new constitutional order.

8.9 WHO DEVELOPS THE GUIDELINES?

The initiation of a process to make or fundamentally revise a constitution is the critical phase where a country sets the rules for its own transformation. Since the way a constitution is made is as important as the resulting content, the starting point must be the conscious decision to develop a consensus-based roadmap for a more just political and social order. The first logical task, after deciding that major reform is necessary, is to develop the guiding principles that will govern the entire process, establishing core expectations regarding integrity and participation.

Who Develops the Guiding Principles? The crucial question of who decides on the guiding principles involves a mix of political negotiation, legal imposition, and popular input. Since constitution-making is intensely political and the stakes are high (determining how power and resources will be shared), the principles often emerge from those already holding power or those negotiating to attain it. However, the best practice is that a committee chosen by all stakeholders must develop the guidelines. This committee can be mandated to regulate its own procedure.

In many post-conflict situations, guiding principles are negotiated among the parties to the conflict and are then included in peace agreements or interim constitutions. In other cases, the local legislature or the government, sometimes after discussion with relevant groups, lays down the principles. Principles may be included in the legislation establishing a constitutional commission or constituent assembly, or in the terms of reference for a parliamentary committee on constitutional development. The Bolivian constituent assembly, for instance, included a committee specifically on the "Vision of the Nation" to develop principles for the rest of the process. When the international community is involved, principles may be laid down in international agreements (like the Bonn Agreement for Afghanistan) or in United Nations decisions. Civil society and political parties also have input, though they usually lack the power to make these principles legally binding themselves.

The diversity of practice reflects the diversity of contexts. There is no single correct answer to who should develop the guidelines, but there are principles that should guide the answer. The process of developing guidelines should itself be inclusive and participatory. It should involve all key stakeholders. It should be transparent, so that everyone can see what principles are being proposed and why. And it should be accountable, so that those who develop the guidelines can be questioned about their choices.

Regardless of who develops them, these principles serve as the terms of reference for the entire process. They are intended to reflect key aspects of the historical context, such as a history of abuse by the state, and broader international norms, like human rights.

The most fundamental principles developed include inclusiveness, participation, transparency, and national ownership. These principles are vital because they assure minority groups whose interests might otherwise be adversely affected by a majority-dominated process, thereby encouraging them to join, rather than undermine, the reform. Moreover, these guidelines influence the content of the final constitution by ensuring the concerns and aspirations of the people, particularly those previously marginalised, are reflected, fostering a sense of national identity and public ownership.

Ultimately, adherence to these principles transforms the constitutional process into a strategic peacebuilding opportunity. While they are typically regarded as political obligations rather than strictly enforceable legal requirements, they are crucial because research indicates that citizens who perceive the consultation process to be insincere lose trust and confidence, not only in the process but in the resulting constitution and their leaders. Therefore, the commitment by the leaders to developing and applying these principles, which may include special measures for public consultation and ensuring women's full participation, is the benchmark for whether a genuine constitutional transformation is taking place.

8.10 CONCLUSION

The preliminary questions addressed in this chapter are not merely technical; they are fundamental to the legitimacy and success of any constitutional review process. The decision whether to undertake a comprehensive review, the design of the roadmap, the holding of a stakeholder conference, the drafting of terms of reference, the composition of a constitutional assembly, and the development of guiding principles all shape the process and its outcome.

Comparative experience offers guidance, but not formulas. Each country must find its own path, adapted to its own circumstances. However, the principles that emerge from comparative experience are clear: inclusivity, participation, transparency, national ownership, and adequate resourcing. Processes that embody these principles are more likely to produce constitutions that are legitimate, durable, and owned by the people.

For Botswana, the lessons are particularly important. The experience of the Dibotelo Commission, operating under the wrong legal framework, illustrates the dangers of getting the preliminary questions wrong. The opportunity now is to get them right: to design a process that rebuilds legitimacy, that includes all voices, that educates and empowers citizens, that produces a constitution for the twenty-first century.

The chapters that follow provide the detailed roadmap for such a process. They trace the phases of review—preparation, consultation, analysis, drafting, adoption—and offer guidance on how each phase should be conducted. But the foundation laid in this chapter is essential. Without clear answers to the preliminary questions, without an inclusive design of the process itself, the later phases cannot succeed. The journey begins here.

RECAP AND TRANSITION

Recap: This chapter has addressed the preliminary questions that must be answered before any constitutional review process can begin. It has examined the fundamental question of whether comprehensive review is needed, drawing on comparative examples from Afghanistan, the Philippines, South Africa, and Kenya. It has explored how law and politics interact in constitution-making. It has been considered who should frame the roadmap, arguing for inclusive involvement of all stakeholders. It has examined the value of a preliminary stakeholder conference, identifying who should attend and what the agenda should cover. It has addressed who should draft the terms of reference, noting the importance of inclusive negotiation. It has defined a constitutional assembly and explored different methods of composition. Finally, it has discussed the guidelines that should govern the process and who should develop them, emphasising the principles of inclusivity, participation, transparency, and national ownership.

Transition: Having established the foundational answers to these preliminary questions, the next chapter turns to the actors who will shape the constitutional process. Chapter Nine examines the role of civil society, political parties, and media in constitution-making. It explores how these actors can contribute to (or undermine) an inclusive and participatory process. It draws on comparative experience from South Africa, Tunisia, Bolivia, Kenya, Egypt, the Philippines, and others to identify best practices and common pitfalls. Understanding the roles and responsibilities of these actors is essential to designing a process that is genuinely participatory and broadly owned.

CHAPTER NINE

THE ROLE OF CIVIL SOCIETY, POLITICAL PARTIES, AND MEDIA IN CONSTITUTION-MAKING

9.1 INTRODUCTION

Contemporary constitution-making processes are commonly presented as exercises in popular participation. Constituent assemblies hold public consultations, constitutional commissions solicit submissions from citizens, and referenda promise that the people will decide their political future. Yet, there is often a significant gap between participation as rhetoric and participation as lived reality. Genuine participation is not measured simply by the number of consultations held or submissions received, but by whether ordinary citizens can meaningfully influence constitutional outcomes.

Comparative experience illustrates this distinction. In South Africa's Eastern Cape, farmworkers gathered in community halls to debate constitutional provisions grounded in their lived experience of apartheid. In Bolivia, indigenous movements mobilised for recognition of a plurinational state. In Tunisia, civil society organisations mediated between political parties that appeared deadlocked. These examples show that constitutions emerge not from abstract principles alone, but from struggles over whose voices are heard, which interests are accommodated, and which visions of political community ultimately prevail.

This chapter examines how three sets of actors shape constitutional outcomes: civil society organisations, political parties, and the media (both traditional and digital). Civil society mobilises participation and provides expertise; political parties negotiate binding constitutional bargains; and media frames constitutional debates and determines which voices reach the public. Drawing on comparative experience from South Africa, Tunisia, Bolivia, Kenya, Namibia, Papua New Guinea, Egypt, and the Philippines, the analysis argues that constitutional legitimacy depends less on elegant institutional design than on the quality and authenticity of the processes that produce it. In an era of social media, algorithmic curation, and coordinated disinformation, genuine participation depends not only on formal procedures but also on the integrity of the information environment in which citizens form preferences and exercise agency.

The actors discussed in this chapter are not peripheral to constitution-making; they are central to its legitimacy and success. Civil society, political parties, and media operate in the space between the formal institutions of the state and the lived realities of citizens. They translate popular concerns into constitutional language, they aggregate interests and negotiate compromises, and they shape the information environment in which constitutional debates unfold. Understanding their roles, their capacities, and their limitations is essential to designing a process that is genuinely participatory and broadly owned.

This chapter examines each set of actors in turn. It explores how civil society organisations can broaden participation, provide expertise, and mediate conflict—and also how they can be marginalised or co-opted. It examines the central role of political parties in negotiating binding constitutional bargains, and the dangers of treating constitution-making as winner-take-all politics. It examines the media's role in shaping constitutional discourse and the new challenges posed by social media, disinformation, and algorithmic amplification. Throughout, it draws on comparative experience to identify best practices and common pitfalls.

9.2 CIVIL SOCIETY ORGANISATIONS

Modern constitutional theory recognises that constitutions drafted behind closed doors by political elites rarely generate the legitimacy required for democratic consolidation. Popular participation has therefore become a normative expectation of contemporary constitution-making. However, how participation functions remains contested. Ordinary citizens may lack the technical language to articulate constitutional visions; their demands may be fragmented or contradictory; and participation risks becoming a ritual that legitimises predetermined outcomes. Civil society organisations (CSOs) act as crucial intermediaries in addressing these challenges, though their role is complex and uneven.

Civil society organisations occupy a unique space in constitution-making. They are not part of the state, so they can speak with independence and critique governmental action. They are not political parties, so they are not directly competing for power and can focus on issues rather than electoral advantage. They are not individuals, so they can aggregate interests, mobilise resources, and sustain engagement over time. These characteristics make them valuable intermediaries between citizens and the formal process.

But civil society is not homogeneous. It includes large, professionalised non-governmental organisations with international connections; small, grassroots community groups with deep local knowledge; trade unions, professional associations, religious bodies, and many others. Each type of organisation has different capacities, different constituencies, and different interests. A well-designed constitutional process must engage with this diversity, creating multiple channels through which different kinds of organisations can participate.

At their best, CSOs broaden participation, translate lived experience into constitutional language, provide technical expertise, and mediate political deadlock. South Africa's 1994–1996 constitution-making process illustrates this capacity. More than two million submissions were made to the Constitutional Assembly, largely due to extensive civil society facilitation. CSOs conducted nationwide consultations, enabling citizens to articulate how apartheid-era injustices shaped their expectations of constitutional change. Experiences of racial discrimination, violence, and exclusion were translated into constitutional commitments to equality, dignity, and human rights.

The South African experience demonstrates the transformative potential of civil society engagement. CSOs did not simply collect submissions; they actively facilitated participation, helping citizens understand constitutional issues and articulate their views. They translated lived experience into constitutional language, connecting personal stories of oppression to structural commitments to equality and dignity. They ensured that the voices of ordinary citizens (farmworkers in the Eastern Cape, women in townships, workers in industrial areas) were heard in the constitutional assembly.

The Women's National Coalition exemplified substantive constitutional engagement. Instead of advocating abstract equality, it built alliances across racial, class, and ideological lines and consulted widely with women across South Africa. The resulting Women's Charter articulated what equality should mean in practice, addressing property rights, family law, political representation, and protection from violence. By grounding constitutional demands in material realities, the coalition prevented equality from becoming a hollow formal guarantee.

The Women's National Coalition is a powerful example of civil society's capacity to shape constitutional content. The coalition brought together women from diverse backgrounds (African, white, Coloured, Indian; urban and rural; professional and working class) to articulate a shared vision of constitutional equality. They consulted widely, listening to women's experiences and concerns. They translated those consultations into concrete constitutional demands, and they lobbied effectively to ensure those demands were included in the final document.

The result was a constitution that addresses gender equality not as an abstract principle, but as a set of concrete commitments: equality in family law, protection from domestic violence, access to reproductive health care, and affirmative measures to address historical disadvantage. These provisions were not the product of elite negotiation; they emerged from grassroots consultation and advocacy. They demonstrate what civil society can achieve when it is organised, inclusive and strategic.

Tunisia provides a different but equally significant example. Following the 2011 revolution, ideological polarisation between the Islamist Ennahda party and secular opposition forces threatened to derail the constitutional process. Civil society intervened decisively through the National Dialogue Quartet, comprising the Tunisian General Labour Union, the Confederation of Industry, Trade and Handicrafts, the Tunisian Human Rights League, and the Order of Lawyers. Possessing credibility across partisan divides, the Quartet mediated negotiations when parties refused direct engagement. Its intervention enabled compromise on contentious issues such as the role of religion, the structure of government, and transitional justice. The 2014 Constitution was passed with an overwhelming majority.

Tunisia's experience illustrates civil society's potential as a mediator in situations of deep political polarisation. When political parties were deadlocked, unable to communicate directly, civil society organisations stepped into the breach. They possessed credibility across partisan lines because they were seen as neutral, as representing broad societal interests rather than narrow political agendas. They had the organisational capacity to facilitate negotiations and the patience to persist through multiple rounds of dialogue.

The Quartet's success was not accidental. It rested on several factors. First, the organisations were independent of political parties and had long histories of advocacy. Second, they represented diverse constituencies (workers, business, human rights advocates, lawyers), giving them broad legitimacy. Third, they were perceived as neutral brokers seeking a constitutional settlement rather than partisan advantage. Fourth, they had the patience and persistence to stay with the process through multiple crises.

Several factors explain the Quartet's effectiveness. The organisations were independent and predated the crisis; they represented diverse constituencies whose support mattered to political actors; and they were perceived as neutral brokers seeking a constitutional settlement rather than partisan advantage. This combination of legitimacy, capacity, and neutrality allowed civil society to stabilise a fragile process.

Bolivia demonstrates civil society's capacity to redefine the political community itself. Indigenous movements, mobilised over decades against marginalisation by Spanish-speaking elites, did not merely seek inclusion in an existing framework. They demanded recognition of Bolivia as a plurinational state. When the constituent assembly was convened in 2006 under Evo Morales, indigenous organisations pressed successfully for constitutional recognition of multiple nations, indigenous autonomy, customary legal systems, gender parity, and state control over natural resources. The 2009 Constitution fundamentally reconceived Bolivian identity, a transformation unimaginable without sustained indigenous mobilisation.

Bolivia's experience shows that civil society can do more than influence constitutional content; it can redefine the very terms of political community. Indigenous movements did not seek simply to be included in a pre-existing framework. They challenged the framework itself, arguing that Bolivia was not a unitary nation, but a plurinational state composed of multiple peoples, each with its own identity, institutions, and rights. This vision, embedded in the 2009 Constitution, transformed Bolivia's understanding of itself.

The success of indigenous movements was the product of decades of organising and mobilisation. They had built strong organisations, developed coherent demands, and cultivated alliances with other social movements. When the constituent assembly convened, they were prepared to engage effectively, to press their case, and to negotiate outcomes. Their experience demonstrates that civil society's influence depends not only on the openness of the process, but also on its own organisational capacity.

Civil society's role, however, is not always effective or positive. Papua New Guinea's independence constitution of 1975 illustrates how weak civil society can limit participation. Although the Constitutional Planning Committee sought to incorporate customary law and conducted consultations across a highly diverse society, low literacy, poor communication infrastructure, and weak civic organisations constrained meaningful engagement. The result was a constitution innovative on paper but poorly understood by the public, functioning more as an elite framework than a widely owned social compact.

Papua New Guinea's experience, although a huge success, offers a cautionary tale. Despite good intentions and extensive consultation, the process failed to generate a broad understanding and ownership because civil society was too weak to translate consultation into genuine participation. Citizens lacked the organisations that could help them understand constitutional issues, articulate their views, and hold the process accountable. The resulting constitution, while innovative in many respects, never achieved the deep legitimacy that comes from broad-based engagement.

The lesson is that civil society cannot be taken for granted. Its capacity must be built, its organisations must be supported, its voices must be amplified. A constitutional process that assumes civil society will simply appear and participate effectively is likely to be disappointed. Investment in civic education, organisational development and outreach is essential.

Egypt highlights civil society's vulnerability to exclusion and co-optation. After Mubarak's fall in 2011, fragmented secular CSOs were outmatched by the organisational strength of the Muslim Brotherhood. The Brotherhood-dominated constituent assembly drafted the 2012 Constitution amid protests and walkouts by women's groups, Christian organisations, and secular NGOs. The constitution collapsed within months following military intervention. The subsequent 2014 process, conducted under military oversight, further marginalised civil society, producing a constitution that entrenched executive and military power despite formal rights protections.

Egypt demonstrates that civil society presence alone does not ensure inclusiveness; effectiveness requires organisational capacity, independence, and legitimacy.

Egypt's experience illustrates the dangers of a weak and fragmented civil society. After the revolution, numerous civil society organisations emerged, but they were small, poorly organised, and lacking in strategic capacity. They were no match for the Muslim Brotherhood, which had decades of organisational experience and a disciplined membership. When the constituent assembly was formed, the Brotherhood dominated, and other voices were excluded or marginalised.

The result was a constitution that lacked broad legitimacy. Women's groups, Christian organisations, and secular NGOs walked out in protest. The constitution was approved in a referendum, but never gained popular acceptance. Within months, it was swept away by military intervention. Egypt's experience shows that civil society presence is not enough; organisations must be strong, independent, and capable of sustained engagement.

The Philippines shows how civil society's role extends beyond drafting to long-term constitutional struggle. Civil society was central to the 1986 People Power Revolution that ended the Marcos dictatorship. However, the 1987 Constitution was drafted by an appointed commission with limited popular consultation. While the constitution entrenched extensive rights protections and limits on executive power, it avoided or diluted difficult distributive questions. Provisions against political dynasties were left to future legislation, allowing entrenched elites to persist. Economic restrictions aimed at preventing oligarchic capture proved rigid and contentious over time. Civil society has since been divided between defending the constitution as a shield against authoritarianism and pressing, often unsuccessfully, for fuller implementation of its transformative promises.

The Philippines' experience highlights that civil society's role does not end with the constitution's adoption. Implementation is as important as drafting, and civil society must continue to press for constitutional promises to be fulfilled. In the Philippines, civil society has been engaged in a long-term struggle to give effect to constitutional provisions that have been neglected or undermined. This struggle continues today, as threats to constitutional democracy re-emerge.

These cases suggest that civil society's constitutional role extends beyond the drafting moment to sustained engagement in implementation and reform. Its effectiveness depends on organisational strength, independence and the ability to translate popular demands into durable constitutional commitments.

9.3 POLITICAL PARTIES

Political parties are central to constitution-making because they possess the organisational capacity to negotiate binding constitutional bargains. They aggregate interests, articulate competing visions, and convert demands into enforceable compromises. Constitution-making succeeds when parties treat the process as distinct from ordinary electoral competition and prioritise constitutional legitimacy over partisan advantage.

Political parties are the primary actors in representative democracy. They organise electoral competition, structure legislative deliberation, and provide citizens with choices about who will govern. In constitution-making, they play an equally central role. They are the organisations through which competing visions of the political community are articulated and negotiated. They have the capacity to make binding commitments on behalf of their members and supporters.

But political parties also pose risks. They may treat constitution-making as an extension of ordinary politics, seeking partisan advantage rather than constitutional legitimacy. They may dominate the process, excluding other voices. They may be unable to reach an agreement when their visions are too far apart. Managing these risks is essential to a successful process.

Kenya's 2010 constitution-making process demonstrates constructive partisan engagement. Following the violent 2007 elections, mediated negotiations produced agreement on comprehensive constitutional reform. The process addressed excessive presidential power, ethnic marginalisation, land grievances and weak institutions. While experts led drafting and consultations, political compromise was essential. Parties accepted devolution to 47 counties, strengthened judicial independence and mechanisms for addressing historical injustices, despite risks to incumbent power. The resulting constitution passed with strong popular support, illustrating how parties can transcend short-term interests to secure stability.

Kenya's experience is instructive. After the violence of 2007, political leaders recognised that the existing constitutional order was unsustainable. They agreed to a process of comprehensive reform, mediated by a panel of eminent persons led by Kofi Annan. Through negotiation, they reached an agreement on a new constitutional framework that addressed many of the grievances that had fuelled conflict.

The key to success was the willingness of parties to accept provisions that limited their own power. Incumbent parties accepted devolution, which dispersed power away from the centre. They accepted a strengthened judiciary, which could review their actions. They accepted mechanisms for addressing historical injustices, which might expose past wrongs. These concessions were not easy, but they were essential to reaching a settlement that could command broad support.

Tunisia offers another example of successful compromise. Despite deep ideological divisions, Ennahda chose accommodation over dominance. It accepted limits on religious provisions, supported robust rights protections, and agreed to a mixed system of government. Secular parties, in turn, accepted recognition of Islam's role in public life. Civil society mediation facilitated these bargains, enabling a constitution acceptable to diverse constituencies.

Tunisia's experience, already discussed in the context of civil society, also illustrates constructive partisan engagement. Ennahda, the Islamist party that won the largest share of votes in post-revolution elections, could have sought to dominate the constitutional process. Instead, it chose accommodation, accepting compromises on issues important to secular parties. This choice reflected strategic calculation (a recognition that a constitution imposed by one party would lack legitimacy), but also a genuine commitment to democratic pluralism.

By contrast, Egypt illustrates the dangers of treating constitution-making as winner-take-all politics. The Muslim Brotherhood interpreted electoral victory as a mandate to dominate drafting, proceeding despite opposition walkouts. The resulting constitution lacked broad legitimacy and collapsed quickly, demonstrating that electoral success alone is insufficient for constitutional authority.

Egypt's experience, also discussed earlier, shows the consequences of partisan overreach. The Muslim Brotherhood, having won elections, acted as if it had a mandate to impose its vision without compromise. It excluded other voices, ignored opposition concerns and pressed ahead with a constitution that reflected its own preferences. The result was a document that lacked legitimacy and quickly collapsed.

The lesson is that electoral victory does not confer the right to dictate constitutional terms. A constitution is not ordinary legislation; it is the framework within which all future legislation will be enacted. It must command broad acceptance across partisan lines, not just majority support. Parties that seek to dominate the process may win in the short term, but they risk losing everything when the constitution they have imposed is rejected.

Bolivia reveals a different risk: dominance by a single transformative movement. The Movement for Socialism used its strength to entrench plurinationalism and redistribution, despite strong regional opposition. Although the constitution was passed by referendum, deep divisions persisted, later contributing to political instability. Even transformative projects require cross-partisan buy-in to endure.

Bolivia's experience illustrates that even well-intentioned transformative projects can generate opposition if they are imposed without sufficient accommodation. The Movement for Socialism had a genuine mandate for change, and the 2009 Constitution reflected important advances in indigenous rights and social justice. But the process also alienated significant segments of the population, particularly in the eastern lowlands, who felt their interests were ignored. These divisions persisted and contributed to subsequent political instability.

The lesson is not that transformative change is impossible, but that it must be pursued through processes that seek to accommodate diverse interests. Even when one party has a clear mandate, it should seek to build the broadest possible consensus. Excluding opponents today creates problems for tomorrow.

Namibia's independence constitution shows how dominance, combined with external pressure, can produce stability at the cost of unresolved justice issues. SWAPO's leadership and international oversight yielded a durable democratic framework with strong rights protections, but debates over land and economic redistribution were deferred, resurfacing later in politics.

Namibia's experience highlights a different trade-off. The independence constitution, negotiated under international supervision, produced a stable democratic framework. But it deferred difficult questions about land and economic redistribution, leaving them to future legislation. These questions have resurfaced repeatedly in subsequent politics, generating ongoing conflict. The lesson is that deferring difficult issues may facilitate agreement in the short term but store up problems for the future.

The Philippines highlights the consequences of a weak, fragmented party system. Parties are often personalistic, fluid, and dominated by dynastic interests. Constitutional reform debates become contests over advantage rather than genuine deliberation. As a result, citizens distrust reform initiatives, even when the constitution's flaws are widely recognised. Without credible parties, constitutional dialogue struggles to gain legitimacy.

The Philippines experience shows how a weak party system can undermine constitutional discourse. When parties are personalistic and fluid, they cannot aggregate interests or articulate coherent visions. When dynastic interests dominate them, they cannot be trusted to pursue the public good. Constitutional reform debates become vehicles for elite advantage rather than genuine deliberation about the common good. Citizens, seeing this, become cynical and disengaged.

9.4 MEDIA AND SOCIAL MEDIA

Constitutional debates unfold not only in formal institutions but within the broader information environment. Traditional media and digital platforms shape which ideas gain traction, whose voices are amplified, and how constitutional stakes are understood.

The media's role in constitution-making is often overlooked but is increasingly important. Media shape what citizens know about the process, what issues they consider important, and what views they encounter. They can educate, inform, and facilitate debate. They can also misinform, polarise, and undermine trust. In an era of social media, these effects are amplified and accelerated.

Traditional media can educate, investigate and provide platforms for debate. In Kenya, radio, television and newspapers played a vital civic education role during the 2010 process, broadcasting hearings and explaining reforms in accessible language. In Tunisia, post-revolution media openness enabled vigorous debate, but also polarisation as outlets aligned with ideological camps.

Traditional media remain important, particularly in countries where internet access is limited. Radio can reach remote and rural communities, providing information in local languages. Newspapers can provide in-depth analysis and investigative reporting. Television can bring constitutional debates into people's homes, making the process visible and accessible.

But traditional media also have limitations. They may be owned by powerful interests that shape coverage to suit their agendas. They may lack the resources for sustained, in-depth coverage of complex constitutional issues. They may be subject to government pressure or control. A healthy information environment requires media that are independent, professional, and committed to public service.

The Philippines illustrates both potentials and limits. Independent media were crucial in mobilising resistance under martial law and educating citizens during the 1987 ratification. Over time, however, media ownership by powerful families has often reduced constitutional debates to personality-driven conflicts, sidelining structural issues.

The Philippines experience shows how media can both enable and constrain constitutional discourse. During the Marcos dictatorship, independent media were essential to resistance, providing information and analysis that could not be obtained elsewhere. During the 1987 ratification, they played a vital educational role. But over time, as media ownership concentrated in powerful families, coverage shifted towards personality and spectacle, away from substantive issues. Constitutional debates became less about structures and rights and more about which personality was up or down.

Social media has transformed constitutional discourse by lowering barriers to participation and enabling rapid mobilisation. Marginalised voices can bypass traditional gatekeepers, but the same platforms facilitate manipulation. Algorithms prioritise emotionally charged content, favouring outrage over nuance. Organised disinformation campaigns, bot networks, and troll farms can manufacture consensus, intimidate critics, and distort public understanding.

Social media offers both promise and peril for constitution-making. The promise: anyone with internet access can participate in constitutional debates, sharing views, organising advocacy, and holding the process accountable. Marginalised groups that lack access to traditional media can find a voice online. Information can spread rapidly, enabling rapid mobilisation.

The peril: the same platforms that enable participation also enable manipulation. Algorithms designed to maximise engagement favour emotionally charged, often misleading content over nuanced analysis. Disinformation campaigns can spread falsehoods faster than they can be corrected. Bot networks can simulate grassroots support or opposition, distorting perceptions of public opinion. Troll farms can intimidate and harass those who express unpopular views.

Kenya's experience shows social media's constructive potential, particularly in mobilising youth and disseminating accurate information during the referendum. Egypt and the Philippines illustrate darker patterns, where coordinated online campaigns amplified polarisation, spread falsehoods, and undermined trust. Influencers with large followings often shape constitutional narratives with limited expertise, while corrections by experts travel more slowly than viral misinformation.

The contrast between Kenya and Egypt/Philippines is instructive. In Kenya, civil society and government used social media effectively to disseminate accurate information and engage citizens. Youth were mobilised through platforms they already used. In Egypt and the Philippines, by contrast, social media became vehicles for polarisation and misinformation, undermining constructive debate.

9.5 IMPLICATIONS FOR CONSTITUTIONAL LEGITIMACY

These dynamics raise fundamental questions about popular participation. If citizen consent is shaped by disinformation or algorithmic manipulation, can it be considered informed? Formal inclusion through consultations and referenda is insufficient if the information environment is deeply distorted.

The legitimacy of constitutional outcomes depends on the quality of the process that produces them. A key dimension of quality is the information environment in which citizens form their views and make their choices. If that environment is polluted by disinformation, manipulation, and polarisation, the resulting consent cannot be considered fully informed.

This is not merely a theoretical concern. In an era of social media, algorithmic amplification, and coordinated disinformation campaigns, the integrity of the information environment cannot be taken for granted. Constitution-makers must attend to it as carefully as they attend to the formal procedures of consultation and drafting.

Comparative experience suggests several responses. Long-term civic education and media literacy are essential to equip citizens to assess information critically. Platform governance must address coordinated inauthentic behaviour while safeguarding free expression. Independent journalism requires protection and support. Diverse channels of engagement, including face-to-face deliberation, can counter online polarisation. Tunisia's National Dialogue demonstrates the value of insulated spaces for negotiation amid digital noise.

Civic education and media literacy are long-term investments. Citizens need the skills to evaluate information sources, to distinguish credible from incredible claims, and to resist manipulation. These skills are not innate; they must be taught and practised. Integrating them into school curricula and adult education programmes is essential.

Platform governance matters. Social media companies make decisions about content moderation, algorithmic amplification, and user verification that shape the information environment. Constitution-makers must engage with these companies, advocating for policies that protect the integrity of constitutional discourse, while respecting free expression.

Independent journalism requires support. In an era of declining revenues and increasing pressure, quality journalism is under threat, yet it remains essential to informed citizenship. Subsidies, non-profit models, and public service broadcasting can help sustain it.

Diverse channels of engagement can counter online polarisation. Face-to-face deliberation has been shown to reduce polarisation and build mutual understanding. Constitutional processes should include opportunities for citizens to engage directly with each other, not only through digital platforms.

9.6 CONCLUSION

Civil society, political parties and media are not peripheral to constitution-making; they are central to its legitimacy. Civil society can empower excluded voices or become marginalised. Political parties can forge inclusive settlements or sabotage processes through domination. The information environment increasingly shapes constitutional outcomes, amplifying both participation and manipulation.

The core challenge of contemporary constitution-making lies not only in institutional design, but in ensuring that citizens can deliberate and decide within a reasonably trustworthy information ecosystem. Genuine participation requires both formal inclusion and conditions that allow citizens to hear credible voices, contest ideas without intimidation, and form judgements free from pervasive manipulation. Building such conditions is long-term, demanding coordinated efforts across education, media, regulation, and civic life. Only then can popular sovereignty remain more than a slogan in the digital age.

The chapter's conclusion returns to the central theme: constitutional legitimacy depends on the quality of participation, and the quality of participation depends on the integrity of the information environment. Civil society, political parties, and media are the key actors in shaping that environment. Their strengths and weaknesses, their capacities and limitations, must be understood and addressed in any constitutional process.

For Botswana, the implications are clear. The constitutional review process must engage actively with civil society, supporting its capacity to facilitate participation and articulate popular demands. It must engage with political parties, encouraging them to treat the process as distinct from ordinary electoral competition and to seek a broad consensus rather than partisan advantage. And it must attend to the information environment, ensuring that citizens have access to accurate information and can participate in genuine deliberation, free from manipulation and distortion.

The chapters that follow provide the detailed roadmap for such a process. They trace the phases of review—preparation, consultation, analysis, drafting, adoption—and offer guidance on how each phase should be conducted. But the foundation laid in this chapter is essential. Without understanding the roles of civil society, political parties, and media, without designing mechanisms that enable their constructive engagement, the later phases cannot succeed.

RECAP AND TRANSITION

Recap: This chapter has examined the roles of three sets of actors in constitution-making: civil society organisations, political parties, and media. It has shown how civil society can broaden participation, translate lived experience into constitutional language, provide expertise, and mediate conflict—drawing on examples from South Africa, Tunisia, Bolivia, Papua New Guinea, Egypt, and the Philippines. It has shown how political parties can forge inclusive settlements or undermine processes through domination, drawing on examples from Kenya, Tunisia, Egypt, Bolivia, Namibia, and the Philippines. And it has shown how media, both traditional and digital, shape the information environment in which constitutional debates unfold, highlighting both the promise of increased participation and the perils of disinformation, polarisation, and manipulation. The chapter has concluded that constitutional legitimacy depends on the quality of participation, and the quality of participation depends on the integrity of the information environment.

Transition: Having examined the key actors who will shape Botswana's constitutional review process, the next chapter turns to the principles that should guide that process. Chapter Ten articulates a set of guiding principles for an inclusive and participatory constitutional review in Botswana. Drawing on international best practice and comparative experience, it sets out principles such as legitimacy, accessibility, inclusivity, transparency, public participation, accountability, independence, consensus-building, respect for human rights, evidence-based approaches, timeliness, civic education, gender sensitivity, sustainability, and deliberation over polarisation. These principles provide the normative framework for the detailed phases that follow.

Chapter Ten

GUIDING PRINCIPLES FOR AN INCLUSIVE AND PARTICIPATORY CONSTITUTIONAL REVIEW PROCESS IN BOTSWANA

10.1 INTRODUCTION

It is important to note that constitutional review is a sensitive undertaking. A model constitutional-making or review process, in line with international best practice, should be both inclusive and participatory. Other equally important principles should be followed. The following principles provide a framework for Botswana's constitutional review process.

The principles articulated in this chapter are not abstract ideals. They are practical requirements drawn from comparative experience and international best practice. They provide the normative framework within which the detailed phases of constitutional review—preparation, consultation, analysis, drafting, adoption—should be designed and implemented. Adherence to these principles does not guarantee success, but departure from them almost guarantees failure.

Each principle is explained below, with attention to its meaning, its rationale, and its implications for Botswana's constitutional review process.

10.2 LEGITIMACY

The process must be seen as widely credible, fair, and owned by the people, not just the government in power. In the context of constitutional review, legitimacy encompasses both procedural legitimacy: the fairness and credibility of the process, and substantive legitimacy: the perceived fairness and appropriateness of the outcome. Procedural legitimacy is especially critical in constitutional reform because the constitution establishes the framework of political power itself. If the process is perceived as imposed, exclusionary, or manipulated, even well-intentioned reforms risk rejection or future instability. By ensuring that citizens recognise the process as fair, representative, and transparent, legitimacy strengthens respect and ownership of the revised constitution.

Legitimacy is the foundation upon which all other principles rest. A constitution that lacks legitimacy may be obeyed out of fear, but it will not command the voluntary allegiance of citizens. It will be vulnerable to challenge when political crises arise, and it will not serve as a shared framework within which conflicts can be peacefully resolved.

Procedural legitimacy concerns the fairness of the process itself. Was the process inclusive? Was it transparent? Were all voices heard? Were decisions made through procedures that participants could accept as fair? Procedural legitimacy does not require that everyone gets everything they want, but it does require that everyone has a fair opportunity to influence outcomes.

Substantive legitimacy concerns the perceived fairness of the outcome. Does the constitution protect fundamental rights? Does it create institutions that are likely to govern justly? Does it reflect the values and aspirations of the people? Substantive legitimacy depends partly on the content of the constitution, but it is also influenced by process. A constitution produced through a fair process is more likely to be perceived as substantively legitimate, even by those who disagree with some of its provisions.

10.3 ACCESSIBILITY

Accessibility refers to the removal of practical, linguistic, physical and informational barriers that prevent effective participation. A process may be formally inclusive, yet functionally inaccessible if citizens cannot understand or engage with it. An accessible process ensures that participation is meaningful rather than symbolic, reinforcing democratic ownership of constitutional reform. Information and venues must be accessible in all major languages, formats (Braille, simple language), and through multiple channels (digital and physical).

Accessibility is about removing barriers. Formal inclusivity (announcing that all are welcome to participate) is not enough if practical obstacles prevent people from actually doing so. These obstacles can be linguistic: if information is only available in English, Setswana-speakers may be excluded; if only in Setswana, minority language speakers may be excluded. They can be physical: if venues are not accessible to persons with disabilities, they are excluded. They can be informational: if materials are written in technical legal language, ordinary citizens cannot understand them. They can be geographic: if consultations are only held in cities, rural communities are excluded.

An accessible process proactively identifies and removes these barriers. It provides information in multiple languages and formats. It holds consultations in accessible venues and reaches out to remote communities. It uses plain language and visual aids to explain constitutional issues. It ensures that all citizens, regardless of their circumstances, have a genuine opportunity to participate.

10.4 INCLUSIVITY

Botswana is characterised by cultural, linguistic, gender, generational, and regional diversity. Groups such as women, youth, persons with disabilities, ethnic minorities, rural communities, and economically marginalised populations have often faced barriers to political participation. An inclusive constitutional review process should:

- Ensure diverse representation in review commissions
- Actively engage marginalised communities through targeted outreach
- Recognise both customary and modern forms of representation

Inclusivity affirms the principle of equality and ensures that constitutional reforms address the lived realities of all citizens, not only dominant groups.

Deliberate efforts must be made to include voices often marginalised: women, youth, ethnic/religious minorities, rural communities, persons with disabilities, and the diaspora. An inclusive process ensures that all voices—women, youth, rural communities, ethnic minorities, and marginalised groups—are represented. International best practice, as seen in South Africa's post-apartheid constitutional drafting, demonstrates that inclusivity prevents alienation and fosters national unity. For Botswana, inclusivity is vital to address historical imbalances and ensure that the constitution reflects the aspirations of every citizen, not just political elites.

Inclusivity goes beyond formal non-discrimination. It requires proactive efforts to reach those who have historically been excluded. Women, for example, have often been marginalised in political processes. An inclusive process ensures that women's voices are heard and their concerns addressed. This may require women-only forums where women can speak freely without intimidation. It may require quotas for women's representation on review commissions. It may require attention to issues that particularly affect women, such as family law, reproductive rights, and protection from violence.

Similarly, youth have often been excluded from constitutional processes, even though they will live with the consequences longest. An inclusive process reaches out to young people through schools, universities, and youth organisations. It creates spaces where young people can articulate their visions for the future. It ensures that the constitution reflects their aspirations and addresses their concerns.

Ethnic and religious minorities, persons with disabilities, rural communities and other marginalised groups all require similar attention. Inclusivity means actively seeking out those who are often overlooked and ensuring that their voices are heard.

10.5 TRANSPARENCY

All information, proposals, and meeting minutes should be publicly accessible. Transparency requires that procedures, objectives, and outcomes of the review be communicated openly. This principle builds trust and prevents suspicion of manipulation. Globally, transparency has been recognised as a safeguard against elite capture, as seen in Chile's ongoing constitutional reform process, where draft texts are made publicly available. In Botswana, transparency would mean taking the people into confidence at every key stage of the constitutional review process, informing and involving the people in key thought processing of the government, publishing draft proposals, broadcasting deliberations, and ensuring citizens can track progress.

Transparency is the antidote to suspicion. When processes are conducted behind closed doors, citizens naturally suspect that deals are being made that serve elite interests rather than the public good. Transparency dispels this suspicion by allowing citizens to see for themselves what is happening.

Transparency operates at multiple levels. At the level of information, it means that all documents (terms of reference, meeting schedules, submissions received, draft proposals) are publicly available. At the level of process, it means that meetings are open to the public and media, or at least that detailed minutes are published. At the level of decision-making, it means that reasons are given for choices made, and that those reasons are accessible and understandable.

Chile's constitutional reform process, mentioned in the source, provides an example. Draft texts are published online, and citizens can comment on them. Deliberations are broadcast, allowing citizens to follow debates. This transparency builds trust and enables informed participation.

10.6 PUBLIC PARTICIPATION

Participation transforms the constitution into a "people's document." International best practice, exemplified by Kenya's 2010 constitutional review, shows that grassroots consultations enhance legitimacy and ownership. For Botswana, structured mechanisms such as town halls, surveys, and community dialogues would empower citizens to shape the supreme law, ensuring that reforms resonate with lived realities.

Public participation is the mechanism through which the other principles, legitimacy, accessibility, inclusivity, and transparency, are given effect. It is not enough that the process is designed to be inclusive and transparent; citizens must actually participate. Their participation must be meaningful, not merely symbolic.

Kenya's 2010 process provides a model. Grassroots consultations were held across the country, reaching even remote communities. Citizens were invited to share their views on constitutional issues, and those views were systematically collected and analysed. The resulting constitution reflected the input received, giving citizens a sense of ownership.

For Botswana, structured mechanisms should be designed to enable broad participation. Town hall meetings allow for face-to-face dialogue between citizens and the commission. Surveys can reach large numbers of people efficiently. Community dialogues, facilitated by local organisations, can enable deeper deliberation. Digital platforms can reach those with internet access, though they must be supplemented by offline methods for those without.

10.7 ACCOUNTABILITY

Accountability ensures that review bodies remain answerable to the public and parliament. This principle prevents abuse of power and guarantees adherence to agreed procedures. Internationally, accountability has been upheld through oversight committees and regular reporting. In Botswana, embedding accountability mechanisms would reassure citizens that partisan interests do not hijack the process.

Accountability means that those who exercise power in the constitutional process must answer for their actions. They must explain their decisions, justify their use of resources, and accept consequences when they fail to meet expectations.

Accountability operates through multiple channels. Oversight committees, composed of representatives from different sectors, can monitor the process and raise concerns. Regular reporting keeps the public and parliament informed of progress and challenges. Independent auditing ensures that resources are used properly. Complaint mechanisms allow citizens to raise concerns about the process and have them addressed.

In Botswana, embedding such mechanisms from the outset would reassure citizens that the process is in safe hands. It would demonstrate that those leading the review take their responsibilities seriously and are willing to be held to account.

10.8 INDEPENDENCE OF THE REVIEW PROCESS

Independence shields the review from political interference. Comparative experience from South Africa and Kenya shows that independent commissions enhance credibility. For Botswana, appointing commissioners from diverse professional and social backgrounds would safeguard impartiality and ensure that reforms are not dictated by ruling party interests alone.

Independence is essential to credibility. If the review body is seen as a tool of the ruling party, its recommendations will be suspect. Citizens will assume that the process is designed to entrench incumbent power rather than to serve the public good.

Independence has multiple dimensions. Structural independence means that the review body is not subordinate to any branch of government. Financial independence means that it has its own budget and is not dependent on executive approval for resources. Personal independence means that commissioners are appointed through processes that insulate them from political pressure and that they have security of tenure.

Diversity in appointments also supports independence. Commissioners drawn from different professional and social backgrounds bring different perspectives and are less likely to be captured by any single interest. They also enhance credibility by demonstrating that the review body represents a range of views.

10.9 CONSENSUS-BUILDING

Consensus-building emphasises broad agreement rather than majoritarian imposition. International best practice highlights that constitutions born of consensus are more durable, as seen in Kenya's 2010 constitution. For Botswana, consensus would reduce polarisation and foster stability, ensuring that contentious issues are resolved through dialogue rather than division.

Constitutions are different from ordinary legislation. Ordinary laws can be passed by majority vote, and those who voted against them must still comply. But a constitution establishes the framework within which all future laws will be made. If a narrow majority imposes it, it will lack the broad acceptance necessary for stability.

Consensus-building seeks to avoid this problem. It emphasises dialogue, negotiation and compromise. It seeks to find common ground among diverse groups. It does not require that everyone agrees on everything, but it does require that the final document is acceptable to a broad range of actors.

Kenya's 2010 constitution exemplifies consensus-building. After decades of conflict and a disputed election that led to violence, political leaders and civil society worked together to forge a constitution that addressed long-standing grievances. The process was not easy, and there were many disagreements. But, through sustained dialogue, a consensus emerged that enabled the constitution to command broad support.

10.10 RESPECT FOR HUMAN RIGHTS AND DEMOCRATIC VALUES

A constitutional review must align with international human rights standards. This principle ensures that fundamental freedoms are protected and democratic identity is strengthened. Botswana's review should embed protections for marginalised groups, including indigenous communities, in line with global norms such as the Universal Declaration of Human Rights.

Human rights are not optional extras; they are fundamental to constitutional democracy. A constitution that fails to protect basic rights—to life, liberty, expression, association, equality—is not worthy of the name. Constitutional review must ensure that the new or revised constitution meets international human rights standards.

This means attending not only to civil and political rights, but also to economic, social, and cultural rights. It means ensuring that marginalised groups—women, children, persons with disabilities, indigenous communities, ethnic and religious minorities—are explicitly protected. It means aligning Botswana's constitution with global norms such as the Universal Declaration of Human Rights, the International Covenant on Civil and Political Rights, and the African Charter on Human and Peoples' Rights.

10.11 EVIDENCE-BASED APPROACH

International best practice emphasises that research, comparative studies, and expert input should inform constitutional reforms. For Botswana, this means commissioning studies on governance, land rights, and electoral systems to ensure reforms are practical and future-oriented. Evidence-based decision-making prevents short-term populism and ensures sustainability.

Constitutional reform is too important to be based on hunches or slogans. It should be informed by evidence: research on how different constitutional arrangements have worked in practice, comparative studies of other countries' experiences, and expert analysis of the likely effects of proposed reforms.

This does not mean that experts should dictate outcomes. Popular participation remains essential, but it is more meaningful when citizens have access to evidence and expert analysis. They can make better judgements about constitutional options when they understand the likely consequences.

For Botswana, this means commissioning studies on key issues before the consultation phase begins. What are the strengths and weaknesses of the current electoral system? How have other countries addressed land rights in their constitutions? What models of devolution might work in Botswana's context? Evidence on these questions can inform both the commission's work and public debate.

10.12 TIMELINESS AND EFFICIENCY

A review process must be structured with clear timelines to avoid stagnation. Internationally, prolonged processes often lead to reform fatigue, as seen in Zimbabwe's drawn-out constitutional reform. Similarly, the constitutional review should not be unduly rushed.

Timeliness and efficiency are about managing the process well. A process that drags on for years can lose momentum. Participants become fatigued, political attention moves elsewhere, and the sense of urgency that drove reform dissipates. Zimbabwe's experience, mentioned in the source, illustrates this danger.

But efficiency should not come at the expense of participation. A process that is rushed to meet an artificial deadline may exclude important voices and produce a constitution that lacks legitimacy. The goal is to be efficient without being hasty—to move steadily through the phases without unnecessary delays, while still allowing adequate time for genuine participation.

Clear timelines, publicly announced and consistently followed, help manage expectations and maintain momentum. They also provide benchmarks against which progress can be measured and accountability enforced.

10.13 CIVIC EDUCATION

Civic education empowers citizens to participate meaningfully. International best practice, such as Uganda's civic education campaigns during its constitutional review, shows that informed citizens contribute constructively. For Botswana, media campaigns, school programmes and community workshops would prevent misinformation and ensure that participation is substantive.

Civic education is the foundation of meaningful participation. Citizens cannot contribute effectively to constitutional debates if they do not understand what a constitution is, why it matters, and what issues are at stake. Civic education provides this foundational knowledge.

South Africa's experience, cited in the source, demonstrates the value of civic education campaigns. Through media, schools, and community programmes, citizens were informed about constitutional issues and empowered to participate. The result was a more informed and engaged public, and a constitution that reflected popular input.

For Botswana, civic education should begin well before consultations start. It should use multiple channels, from radio, television, print, social media, schools, and community workshops, to reach all citizens. It should be available in all major languages and accessible formats. It should explain not only the content of constitutional issues but also the process through which citizens can participate.

10.14 GENDER SENSITIVITY

Gender sensitivity ensures that women's voices are central. International best practice recognises gender equality as a cornerstone of democratic constitutions, as seen in South Africa's emphasis on women's representation. For Botswana, quotas for women in review committees and deliberate inclusion of gender perspectives would address historical imbalances and promote equality.

Gender sensitivity is not an add-on; it is central to constitutional legitimacy. Women make up half the population, yet their voices have historically been marginalised in constitutional processes. A constitution produced without women's full participation cannot claim to represent the people.

South Africa's experience demonstrates what is possible. Women's organisations mobilised effectively, built alliances across racial and class lines, and pressed their demands. The resulting constitution includes strong protections for gender equality and provisions addressing issues of particular concern to women.

For Botswana, gender sensitivity requires deliberate measures. Quotas for women's representation on review commissions ensure that women are at the table. Women-only forums create spaces where women can speak freely without intimidation. Gender analysis of all proposals ensures that the impact on women is considered. Outreach to women's organisations ensures that their expertise is drawn upon.

10.15 SUSTAINABILITY

Sustainability requires that reforms anticipate future challenges and remain adaptable. International best practice encourages mechanisms for periodic review to prevent constitutional crises. For Botswana, embedding provisions for scheduled constitutional reviews would ensure resilience and adaptability in a rapidly changing world.

A constitution must be durable enough to provide stability, but flexible enough to adapt to changing circumstances. Sustainability is about striking this balance. A constitution that is too rigid may become obsolete, unable to address new challenges. A constitution that is too flexible may lose its character as fundamental law, becoming just another set of rules that can be changed at will.

Mechanisms for periodic review can help maintain this balance. By providing for regular, scheduled reviews, a constitution can be updated to reflect changed circumstances without requiring the extraordinary effort of a full-scale constitutional process. These reviews can be more limited in scope, addressing specific issues, rather than reopening the entire constitutional settlement.

For Botswana, embedding such provisions would ensure that the constitution remains relevant and resilient. It would prevent the accumulation of pressures that lead to a crisis. It would demonstrate foresight and a commitment to long-term constitutional health.

10.16 DELIBERATION OVER POLARISATION

A properly conducted constitutional review process must value deliberation over polarisation. Deliberation emphasises reasoned dialogue, mutual respect, and collective problem-solving. Unlike polarised debate, which frames issues as zero-sum conflicts, deliberation seeks common ground and informed consensus. Deliberative processes enhance the quality of decision-making by encouraging reflection, compromise, and understanding of competing perspectives.

Botswana's governance tradition places a strong emphasis on consultation and consensus. The kgotla system exemplifies deliberative democracy by prioritising dialogue over confrontation. In the constitutional review context, prioritising deliberation helps:

- Reduce political and social polarisation
- Build shared understanding of constitutional issues
- Foster long-term acceptance of reform outcomes

Structured deliberative forums, moderated discussions and civic education can help sustain a respectful and constructive process.

Deliberation is about how we talk to each other. In a polarised debate, the goal is to defeat the other side. Arguments are weapons, and compromise is weakness. In deliberation, the goal is to solve problems together. Arguments are contributions to collective understanding, and compromise is how we find common ground.

Botswana's kgotla tradition embodies deliberative values. In the kgotla, community members gather to discuss matters of common concern. Everyone has a chance to speak. The goal is not to win a vote, but to reach a consensus that all can accept. This tradition provides cultural resources for designing a deliberative constitutional process.

In practice, deliberation requires structured forums where citizens can engage with each other respectfully. It requires skilled moderators who can facilitate dialogue and manage conflict. It requires information that participants can use to inform their judgements. It requires time, as deliberation cannot be rushed.

10.17 CONCLUSION

By grounding the review process in the above principles, Botswana can ensure that the constitutional review process reflects the will and aspirations of the people. These principles are not abstract ideals but practical requirements for democratic governance and social cohesion. Ultimately, an inclusive and participatory constitutional review process strengthens not only the constitution itself, but also the democratic culture upon which Botswana's future depends.

Botswana's constitutional review is a historic opportunity to deepen democracy and strengthen national unity. By adhering to principles of inclusivity, transparency, participation, accountability, independence, consensus-building, respect for human rights, evidence-based decision-making, timeliness, civic education, gender sensitivity, and sustainability, Botswana can align its process with international best practice. Ultimately, these principles ensure that the constitution is not merely a legal document but a living covenant between the state and its people.

The principles articulated in this chapter are not a checklist to be ticked off and forgotten. They are commitments that must be woven into the fabric of the process at every stage. They require constant attention, constant effort, constant renewal. But the payoff is immense: a constitution that the people truly own, that commands their allegiance, that can endure through crises and changes.

Botswana has a historic opportunity. The constitutional review process, if designed and implemented according to these principles, can deepen democracy, strengthen national unity and produce a constitution for the twenty-first century. The principles provide the roadmap; the chapters that follow provide the detailed directions.

RECAP AND TRANSITION

Recap: This chapter has articulated fifteen guiding principles for Botswana's constitutional review process: legitimacy, accessibility, inclusivity, transparency, public participation, accountability, independence, consensus-building, respect for human rights, evidence-based approach, timeliness and efficiency, civic education, gender sensitivity, sustainability, and deliberation over polarisation. Each principle has been explained with reference to its meaning, its rationale, and its implications for Botswana. Together, these principles provide the normative framework within which the detailed phases of constitutional review should be designed and implemented.

Transition: Having established the guiding principles that should inform Botswana's constitutional review, the next chapter turns to the first phase of the process itself. Chapter Eleven examines **Foundation and Preparation (Phase I)**. It explores how to establish the political mandate and legal enabling framework, how to create an independent Constitutional Review Commission or Assembly, and how to prepare for civic education and public engagement. This phase lays the groundwork for everything that follows; getting it right is essential to the success of the entire enterprise.

Chapter Eleven

FOUNDATION AND PREPARATION

11.1 INTRODUCTION

A constitution-making or constitutional review process provides a critical opportunity for a nation to build consensus around its fundamental values, institutional arrangements, and vision for governance. At the heart of most debates about constitutional reform lies not only the substance of the constitution itself, but the way the process is conducted. Experience from comparative constitutional practice demonstrates that legitimacy is shaped less by the elegance of constitutional text and more by the credibility, inclusiveness, and transparency of the process that produces it.

The Foundation and Preparation phase (Phase I) is therefore indispensable. This phase establishes the political, legal, and institutional framework that enables a constitutional review to proceed in a legitimate and orderly manner. It is during this stage that trust is built, expectations are managed, and the conditions for meaningful public participation are created. Weak foundations almost invariably undermine later phases, regardless of the quality of drafting or consultation undertaken thereafter.

Comparative experience from countries such as South Africa (1996), Kenya (2010) and Namibia (1990) illustrates how a carefully designed Phase I can produce stable and widely respected constitutional outcomes. Conversely, experiences in Zambia, Tanzania and Zimbabwe (2013) show how elite-driven mandates, politicised commissions, vague enabling legislation and weak civic education can erode public confidence and stall or delegitimise reform efforts.

Phase I typically spans three to six months, though countries facing complex political dynamics, geographical challenges or limited resources may require a longer timeframe. Importantly, this phase is not concerned with drafting constitutional provisions; rather, it focuses on establishing the legal and institutional architecture for a credible process.

The Foundation and Preparation phase is the most critical, yet often most neglected stage of constitutional review. There is a natural impulse to move quickly to the visible work of consultation and drafting, to show progress and generate momentum. But this impulse must be resisted. The work of Phase I is invisible, but essential. It is the groundwork upon which everything else depends.

Three interrelated components define Phase I:

1. The establishment of a political mandate and the enactment of a legal enabling framework.

2. The creation of an independent Constitutional Review Commission or Constituent Assembly.

3. Civic education and preparation of materials to enable informed public participation.

This chapter examines each of these components through comparative analysis and concludes with practical recommendations for completing Phase I, with relevance to Botswana and its Members of Parliament.

11.2 KEY COMPONENTS OF PHASE I

11.2.1 Political Mandate and Legal Enabling Act

11.2.1.1 Establishing a Political Mandate

Every constitutional review process begins with a political decision to initiate reform. This political mandate provides the authority and legitimacy necessary for the process to commence. Without it, constitutional reform remains aspirational and vulnerable to obstruction or reversal.

Political mandates are typically expressed through parliamentary resolutions, executive proclamations, negotiated political agreements, or transitional arrangements. In post-conflict or transitional settings, mandates may also emerge from peace agreements or internationally brokered settlements. Regardless of form, the mandate must reflect genuine political willingness, particularly from dominant political actors whose interests are most directly affected by constitutional change.

Constitution-making is inherently political. While technical expertise is essential, political elites ultimately decide whether reform proceeds and under what conditions. In South Africa (1996) and Kenya (2010), broad political negotiations between rival parties generated sufficient consensus to sustain lengthy and contentious reform processes. In both cases, political actors recognised that constitutional legitimacy required compromise and restraint.

A credible political mandate performs several functions. It anchors the process in law, ensures continuity across political cycles, clarifies scope and objectives, and provides assurance to civil society, donors, and the public that the process will be respected. Where political will is absent or fragmented, constitutional reform is easily delayed, contested or captured.

The importance of a genuine political mandate cannot be overstated. A process that lacks political backing from key actors will struggle to gain traction. Decisions made by the review body may be ignored, resources may be withheld, and the process may be undermined at critical junctures. Conversely, a process with broad political support can weather controversies and maintain momentum through inevitable difficulties.

In Botswana's context, securing a political mandate means engaging all political parties represented in Parliament, not just the ruling party. It means building consensus across partisan lines about the need for review and the basic parameters of the process. The experience of the Dibotelo Commission, initiated by executive action alone, illustrates the dangers of a mandate that is too narrow. A genuinely inclusive mandate, by contrast, would signal that the review belongs to the nation as a whole, not to any particular party or faction.

11.2.1.2 Enacting a Constitutional Review Act

While the political mandate signals intent, the Constitutional Review Act (CRA) establishes the legal machinery through which reform is conducted. The CRA serves as the backbone of the process, defining institutions, powers, procedures, timelines, funding arrangements, and mechanisms for adoption.

Scholars note that constitution-making unfolds in stages resembling ordinary legislative processes, preceded by an "idea-generating stage" in which interests mobilise and parameters are set. The CRA institutionalises this stage, transforming political agreement into enforceable legal obligations.

A robust CRA should specify:

- The objectives and scope of the review
- The duration and sequencing of phases
- Budgetary provisions and financial autonomy
- The establishment, composition and powers of an independent review body
- Procedures for public participation and reporting
- The final method of adoption (referendum, parliamentary approval, or both)

Weak or vague enabling legislation creates ambiguity, invites politicisation, marginalises civil society, and exposes the process to legal challenges. Comparative experience consistently shows that detailed and transparent legal frameworks strengthen legitimacy and resilience.

The Constitutional Review Act is the legal foundation of the entire process. It must be drafted with care, anticipating potential challenges and building in safeguards against capture and manipulation. It should be developed through inclusive consultation, not imposed by the executive alone, and it should be enacted by Parliament, giving it the legitimacy that comes from representative approval.

Key provisions deserve particular attention. The objectives and scope of the review should be clearly stated, so that everyone understands what the process is intended to achieve and what issues are on the table. The duration and sequencing should be realistic, allowing adequate time for each phase while maintaining momentum. Budgetary provisions should ensure financial autonomy, so that the review body is not dependent on executive discretion for resources.

The establishment, composition and powers of the review body are discussed in the next section. Procedures for public participation and reporting should be specified in detail, so that citizens know how they can engage and how their input will be used. And the final method of adoption should be decided at the outset, so that everyone knows what standard must be met for the new constitution to come into force.

11.2.1.3 Comparative Experience

South Africa's process was anchored in a negotiated political settlement that culminated in the Interim Constitution of 1993. This document established constitutional principles binding on the final constitution and created a Constitutional Assembly with clear authority, timelines, and participation obligations. Judicial oversight by the Constitutional Court further reinforced legality and credibility.

Namibia's 1990 Constitution emerged from a negotiated independence settlement and elections to a Constituent Assembly. Although elite-driven, the process derived legitimacy from the inclusive nature of the negotiations and the subsequent electoral mandate.

Kenya's reform journey (2000–2010) was contentious, but ultimately stabilised through the Constitution of Kenya Review Act. The Act embedded principles negotiated between government and civil society, established clear procedures, and mandated public participation.

By contrast, Zambia's repeated reform efforts faltered due to inconsistent mandates, politicised appointments, and weak consensus. Tanzania's process suffered from executive dominance in appointments and unresolved political contestation, leading to a loss of momentum. Zimbabwe's 2013 process, though legally structured, was heavily shaped by political control, raising concerns about inclusivity and impartiality.

These experiences demonstrate that strong political mandates, combined with detailed enabling legislation, produce the most legitimate outcomes, while executive-dominated and ambiguous frameworks undermine trust.

The comparative examples are instructive. South Africa's combination of political negotiation, clear legal framework, and judicial oversight produced a constitution that is widely admired. Kenya's process, though contentious, ultimately succeeded because the enabling Act embedded principles that had been negotiated between government and civil society. Namibia's process, while elite-driven, maintained legitimacy through inclusive negotiations and an electoral mandate.

The negative examples are equally instructive. Zambia's repeated failures show the consequences of weak mandates and politicised processes. Tanzania's stalled reform demonstrates how executive dominance can derail even well-intentioned efforts. Zimbabwe's experience reveals that a legally structured process can still be undermined by political control.

For Botswana, the lesson is clear: invest heavily in getting Phase I right. Secure a broad political mandate. Enact a detailed, transparent Constitutional Review Act. Learn from both the successes and failures of others.

11.2.2 Establishment of an Independent Constitutional Review Commission or Assembly

Once a political mandate and legal framework are in place, an independent body must be established to manage the process. This may take the form of an Independent Constitutional Review Commission (ICRC) or a Constituent Assembly.

A Constituent Assembly is typically elected or specially convened to draft and adopt a constitution, after which it dissolves. An ICRC, by contrast, often focuses on consultation, analysis and drafting proposals for adoption by another body. Both models aim to insulate constitution-making from ordinary partisan politics.

Elster argues that constitutions should be drafted by specially convened bodies rather than ordinary legislatures, in order to reduce institutional self-interest. In practice, constitution-making bodies vary widely in composition and function, including expert commissions, transitional legislatures, national conferences, or hybrid arrangements.

The effectiveness of a commission or assembly depends less on its label and more on its independence, inclusiveness, and clarity of mandate.

The choice between a commission and an assembly involves trade-offs. A commission can be smaller, more expert, and more focused, but it may lack democratic legitimacy. An assembly can be more representative, but it may be unwieldy and subject to partisan dynamics. Hybrid models, such as a commission that drafts and an assembly that approves, can combine the advantages of both.

What matters most is not the form, but the substance. The body must be independent, free from control by the executive or any political party. It must be inclusive (representative of the diversity of the nation, and its mandate must be clear), so that everyone understands what it is supposed to do and what limits apply.

11.2.2.1 Importance of Independence and Inclusivity

A constitutional review body is often expected to symbolise national unity. Its members should, therefore, be respected, broadly representative and non-partisan. Inclusivity may be achieved through proportional representation, transparent appointments, or sectoral nominations.

Independence is critical. Appointment procedures should involve multiple actors, including opposition parties and civil society, and be conducted transparently. Financial and operational autonomy must also be guaranteed.

As Ghai observes, the legitimacy of a constituent body lies in its inclusiveness. Decisions must be grounded in public input and technical expertise, rather than partisan interests.

Independence and inclusivity are mutually reinforcing. An inclusive body is more likely to be independent because its members come from diverse backgrounds and owe allegiance to different constituencies. No single interest can dominate. Conversely, an independent body is better able to be inclusive because it is not beholden to those who would exclude certain voices.

Appointment procedures must be designed to secure both qualities. They should involve multiple actors: the President, Parliament, the judiciary, civil society, etc., to prevent any single actor from controlling the outcome. They should be transparent so that the public can see who is being considered and why. They should seek out individuals who are respected for their integrity, expertise, and commitment to the public good.

11.2.2.2 Comparative Experience

South Africa's Constitutional Assembly (1994–1996) operated under constitutional principles and judicial oversight, incorporating extensive public submissions. Kenya's Committee of Experts functioned as a technically skilled, independent body responsible for harmonising drafts and managing contentious issues.

However, Kenya's broader process became unwieldy due to the size of the National Constitutional Conference, affecting coherence. Namibia's Constituent Assembly, though elite-driven, derived legitimacy from elections and consensus.

In Zambia, Tanzania and Zimbabwe, executive dominance, inconsistent structures and limited independence undermined public trust.

South Africa's Constitutional Assembly combined representative legitimacy with technical expertise. It was composed of members of Parliament who had electoral mandates, but it operated under constitutional principles and judicial oversight that constrained partisan discretion. Extensive public submissions ensured that popular voices were heard.

Kenya's Committee of Experts was a different model: a small, technically skilled body, responsible for harmonising drafts and managing contentious issues. It operated alongside a larger, more representative National Constitutional Conference. This hybrid approach combined technical expertise with broad representation, though the Conference's size sometimes affected coherence.

The negative examples reinforce the importance of independence. In Zambia, Tanzania and Zimbabwe, executive dominance and limited independence undermined public trust. The review bodies were seen as tools of those in power, not as neutral arbiters of the public interest.

11.2.3 Civic Education and Preparation of Materials

11.2.3.1 Civic Education

Meaningful public participation is impossible without public understanding. Civic education prepares citizens to engage with constitutional issues by explaining what a constitution is, why reform is occurring, and how participation can occur.

Modern constitution-making increasingly recognises civic education as integral. Effective programmes use multiple platforms, from radio, print, community forums, and digital media, and should be delivered in all major local languages.

Civic education must be non-partisan and inclusive, reaching women, youth, rural populations, minorities, and persons with disabilities. It should be continuous, rather than episodic, fostering a culture of constitutionalism and democratic engagement.

Civic education is not a luxury; it is a necessity. Without it, participation becomes a ritual rather than a genuine exercise in democratic decision-making. Citizens may attend consultations, but they will not understand the issues well enough to contribute meaningfully. Their voices will be absent from the constitutional conversation.

Effective civic education uses multiple channels because different populations access information in different ways. Radio reaches remote rural communities. Television reaches urban audiences. Print materials can be distributed through schools and community centres. Digital media can engage youth. Community forums enable face-to-face dialogue. All should be used.

Civic education must be available in all major local languages. Citizens cannot engage with constitutional issues if they cannot understand the information provided. Translation and interpretation services are essential.

And civic education must be continuous, not a one-off event. Understanding develops over time, through repeated exposure and discussion. A sustained campaign, running throughout the review process, is more effective than a few scattered programmes.

11.2.3.2 Preparation of Materials

Preparation involves developing accessible materials and mechanisms for collecting public input. Draft constitutions may be published for public debate, supported by expert analysis and simplified guides.

Independent commissions often manage these preparatory tasks, including analysing submissions and preparing draft texts for consideration by decision-making bodies.

Materials must be accessible. Simplified guides explain constitutional concepts in plain language. Translations make information available to all linguistic communities. Visual aids, such as diagrams and infographics, can help convey complex ideas. Braille and audio formats ensure access for persons with visual impairments.

Mechanisms for collecting public input must also be prepared. Submission forms, online portals, suggestion boxes, and other tools should be designed and tested before consultations begin. Staff must be trained to receive and record submissions accurately. Systems for tracking and analysing submissions must be established.

11.2.3.3 Comparative Experience

South Africa's civic education campaign was extensive and inclusive, resulting in over two million public submissions. Kenya combined strong civic education with technical oversight by the Committee of Experts. Namibia's process, while elite-driven, maintained credibility through political consensus and a strong rights focus.

South Africa's experience demonstrates what is possible with sustained investment in civic education. The campaign reached millions of citizens, explaining constitutional issues and encouraging participation. The result, over two million submissions, was a testament to the effectiveness of the effort.

Kenya's experience shows how civic education can be combined with technical oversight. The Committee of Experts provided expert analysis and drafting, while civic education campaigns ensured that citizens understood the issues and could participate meaningfully.

Namibia's process, while more elite-driven, maintained credibility through political consensus and a strong focus on rights. The lesson is that different approaches can work in different contexts, but civic education consistently enhances legitimacy.

11.3 CONCLUDING REMARKS

The Foundation and Preparation phase determines whether constitutional reform can proceed credibly. Political willingness, legal clarity, institutional independence and informed public participation form the pillars of legitimacy.

An independent review body, supported by comprehensive civic education, enables citizens to engage meaningfully and ensures that reform reflects national priorities rather than partisan interests.

Phase I is the foundation upon which everything else rests. If the foundation is weak, the entire structure is at risk. If the foundation is strong, the process can weather the inevitable challenges and controversies that arise.

The pillars of legitimacy—political willingness, legal clarity, institutional independence, informed public participation—must all be present. A missing pillar weakens the entire structure. Political willingness without legal clarity leaves the process vulnerable to challenge. Legal clarity without institutional independence leaves the process vulnerable to capture. Institutional independence without informed public participation leaves the process disconnected from the people.

11.4 RECOMMENDATIONS FOR PHASE I

Key recommendations include:

- Securing a broad political mandate through inclusive dialogue.
- Enacting a detailed Constitutional Review Act.
- Establishing an independent, representative review body.
- Implementing comprehensive civic education before consultations.
- Building operational systems for participation.
- Ensuring transparency and accountability throughout.

Comparative experience demonstrates that successful constitutional reform begins not with drafting, but with careful preparation. Phase I must, therefore, be approached as a foundational investment in legitimacy, trust, and democratic governance.

Each recommendation deserves careful attention.

Securing a broad political mandate means engaging all political parties, not just the ruling party. It means building consensus across partisan lines about the need for review and the basic parameters of the process. It means ensuring that the mandate is not just formal, but genuine—that political actors are truly committed to the process and its outcomes.

Enacting a detailed Constitutional Review Act means drafting legislation that specifies objectives, scope, duration, sequencing, budget, institutional arrangements, participation procedures and adoption mechanisms. It means developing this legislation through inclusive consultation and enacting it through Parliament.

Establishing an independent, representative review body means designing appointment procedures that involve multiple actors, ensuring financial and operational autonomy, and selecting members who are respected for their integrity, expertise and commitment to the public good.

Implementing comprehensive civic education before consultations means investing in programmes that reach all citizens, using multiple channels and languages, and providing accessible information about constitutional issues and the process of participation.

Building operational systems for participation means developing submission mechanisms, training staff, establishing tracking and analysis systems, and ensuring that all systems are tested and ready before consultations begin.

Ensuring transparency and accountability throughout means publishing all documents, opening meetings to public scrutiny, providing regular reports and establishing mechanisms for citizens to raise concerns and have them addressed.

RECAP AND TRANSITION

Recap: This chapter has examined the Foundation and Preparation phase (Phase I) of constitutional review. It has explored three key components: establishing a political mandate and enacting a legal enabling framework; creating an independent Constitutional Review Commission or Assembly; and conducting civic education and preparing materials for public engagement. It has drawn on comparative experience from South Africa, Kenya, Namibia, Zambia, Tanzania, and Zimbabwe to identify best practices and common pitfalls. It has been concluded that Phase I is foundational: weak foundations undermine later phases, while strong foundations enable legitimate and credible processes. Recommendations for Phase I include securing a broad political mandate, enacting a detailed Constitutional Review Act, establishing an independent and representative review body, implementing comprehensive civic education, building operational systems for participation, and ensuring transparency and accountability throughout.

Transition: Having established the foundation through Phase I, the next chapter turns to a deeper examination of one of its most critical components. Chapter Twelve focuses exclusively on **Civic Education**. It explores the theoretical foundations of civic education in constitutional processes, drawing on scholars such as Balkin, McClain, Fleming, Black, and Jackson. It examines comparative experiences from South Africa, Kenya, Bolivia, and the Philippines and draws out lessons for Botswana. Understanding why civic education matters and how to do it well is essential to ensuring that Phase I achieves its goals.

CHAPTER TWELVE

CIVIC EDUCATION

12.1 INTRODUCTION

Civic education must precede a comprehensive constitutional process. This assertion rests on solid logic. There is no point in asking people to give their views on anything they don't understand.

Across the diverse experiences of South Africa, Kenya, Bolivia, and the Philippines, a striking convergence emerges: civic education operates as both the *medium* and the *measure* of democratic constitutionalism. Each case demonstrates that the success of constitutional reform depends less on the elegance of institutional design than on the capacity of citizens to understand, internalise, and defend the constitutional principles that govern them. When examined through the theoretical frameworks of Jack M. Balkin, Linda C. McClain and James E. Fleming, Derek W. Black, and Vicki C. Jackson, these empirical experiences reveal the same normative truth: constitutionalism is sustained not by text alone, but by civic learning, reflective engagement, and institutional participation.

Civic education is not merely a preliminary step to be checked off before the "real" work of consultation and drafting begins. It is an ongoing process that runs through every phase of constitutional review. It is the means by which citizens become equipped to participate meaningfully. It is also an end in itself: a citizenry that understands its constitution and is committed to its principles is the best guarantee of constitutional endurance.

This chapter examines civic education through both theoretical and comparative lenses. It draws on the work of leading scholars to explain why civic education is essential to constitutionalism. It examines the experiences of South Africa, Kenya, Bolivia and the Philippines to identify what works and what does not. And it draws out lessons for Botswana's constitutional review process.

12.2 CIVIC EDUCATION AS THE ANTIDOTE TO CONSTITUTIONAL ROT

Jack Balkin's concept of *constitutional rot*: the erosion of civic virtue, public trust, and institutional accountability, provides a powerful lens for understanding the role of civic education. South Africa's Truth and Reconciliation Commission (TRC) serves as a prime example of a powerful yet limited intervention. It provided a crucial national catharsis and, through its public hearings, acted as a profound, if temporary, form of civic pedagogy. However, its legacy is debated; it was not designed as a sustained curriculum, and South Africa continues to struggle with the deep-seated socio-economic inequalities the TRC sought to address, demonstrating that even monumental efforts cannot single-handedly inoculate a society against constitutional decay. This highlights the critical importance of enduring mechanisms.

Constitutional rot, in Balkin's formulation, refers to the process by which a constitutional order loses its vitality. Civic virtue declines. Public trust erodes. Institutional accountability weakens. The forms of constitutional government may remain, but the substance drains away. Citizens become cynical, disengaged, and susceptible to demagoguery.

Civic education is the antidote to constitutional rot. It cultivates the civic virtues—attentiveness, deliberation, tolerance, public-spiritedness—that sustain constitutional government. It builds public trust by demonstrating that institutions are worthy of trust. It strengthens accountability by equipping citizens to monitor and challenge their government.

South Africa's Truth and Reconciliation Commission was a powerful intervention, but it was not sustained. It provided a moment of national catharsis and civic learning, but it did not create ongoing mechanisms for civic education. As a result, its effects have faded over time, and South Africa continues to struggle with the legacy of apartheid and the challenges of building a unified democratic culture.

The lesson for Botswana is that civic education must be enduring, not episodic. It must be built into the fabric of the constitutional process and, ultimately, into the ongoing life of the constitutional order.

In Kenya, sustained grassroots forums have provided citizens with a practical, ongoing education in navigating post-authoritarian devolution and demanding accountability. Similarly, Bolivia's intercultural assemblies have made consistent strides in challenging historical exclusion by embedding indigenous epistemologies into the fabric of governance.

The peril of neglecting a sustained approach to civic education is starkly visible in the Philippines. There, episodic and fragmented civic education has created a dangerous vacuum. This vacuum has been eagerly filled by a resilient culture of patronage and a torrent of digital disinformation. These forces actively exploit an underdeveloped civic culture to fuel populist resurgence, structurally threatening democratic stability and undermining the constitutional ideal of an independent, critically engaged citizenry.

Kenya's experience demonstrates the value of sustained grassroots engagement. Civic education did not end with the constitutional process; it continued through ongoing forums in which citizens learned to navigate the new devolved system and hold their leaders accountable. This ongoing education has helped embed constitutional principles in everyday practice.

Bolivia's experience shows how civic education can be transformative when it incorporates indigenous epistemologies. By recognising and valuing indigenous ways of knowing, the constitutional process helped challenge historical patterns of exclusion and build a more inclusive political community.

The Philippines offers a cautionary tale. Episodic civic education (a burst of activity around the constitutional process, then nothing) created a vacuum. Into that vacuum flowed patronage politics and digital disinformation, exploiting an underdeveloped civic culture and threatening democratic stability. The lesson is clear: civic education must be sustained, not episodic.

Across these cases, civic education emerges not as a supplement but as the corrective mechanism that interrupts cycles of decay and enables renewal.

12.3 FROM PATRIOTIC EDUCATION TO REFLECTIVE PATRIOTISM

Linda McClain and James Fleming distinguish between *patriotic education*, which risks indoctrination, and *reflective patriotism*, which confronts historical injustice as a condition for genuine belonging. South Africa exemplifies reflective patriotism by embedding reconciliation and human dignity into civic curricula. Kenya's civic education addressed ethnic violence directly, teaching citizens to deliberate across group boundaries. Bolivia's plurinational reforms reframed national identity through intercultural education, turning constitutional learning into cultural recovery. The Philippines, however, leaned toward celebratory narratives of People Power without embedding critical reflection, leaving citizens vulnerable to nostalgic authoritarianism.

Comparative evidence suggests that reflective patriotism, not uncritical loyalty, is the pedagogical foundation of inclusive constitutionalism.

The distinction between patriotic education and reflective patriotism is crucial. Patriotic education teaches uncritical loyalty: love of country without question, celebration without critique. It risks indoctrination and can be used to suppress dissent and justify injustice. Reflective patriotism, by contrast, teaches love of country that is compatible with critical engagement. It acknowledges historical injustices and ongoing failures. It insists that genuine belonging requires working to make the country better, not simply celebrating it as it is.

South Africa's approach exemplifies reflective patriotism. Civic curricula address the realities of apartheid, not to wallow in guilt, but to understand the past and commit to a different future. Reconciliation and human dignity are central themes. Students learn that being South African means confronting the past and building a society based on equality and respect.

Kenya's civic education addressed ethnic violence directly. After the trauma of 2007–2008, it was essential to help citizens understand what had happened and how to prevent it from happening again. Civic education taught deliberation across group boundaries, building the skills and dispositions necessary for a multi-ethnic democracy.

Bolivia's intercultural education reframed national identity. Instead of a single, homogeneous nation, Bolivia was reconceived as plurinational, composed of multiple peoples with distinct identities and rights. Civic education became a form of cultural recovery, helping indigenous communities reclaim their histories and traditions.

The Philippines, by contrast, leaned towards celebratory narratives. People Power was celebrated as a moment of national unity, but there was little critical reflection on what had gone wrong and what still needed fixing. This left citizens vulnerable to nostalgic appeals to authoritarianism, as seen in the resurgence of support for strongman politics.

12.4 EDUCATION AS A CONSTITUTIONAL RIGHT AND FOUNDATION OF REPUBLICAN GOVERNMENT

Derek Black's argument that education is constitutionally mandated as a prerequisite for republican self-rule finds resonance across all four cases.

South Africa's 1996 Constitution enshrines a justiciable right to basic education (Article 29), framing it as a foundation for political equality. Similarly, Kenya's 2010 Constitution guarantees free and compulsory basic education (Article 53), creating a concrete, enforceable state obligation.

In contrast, Bolivia's 2009 Constitution takes a more transformative approach, defining education as "unitary, public, universal, democratic, participatory, decolonising, and intercultural" (Article 78). This is less a specific right than a declarative philosophy aimed at fundamentally restructuring the state's relationship with indigenous knowledge and power.

The Philippine case underscores the limitation of constitutional text alone. While its 1987 Constitution mandates quality education (Article XIV, Section 1), this has functioned as an aspirational principle rather than a justiciable right, with implementation failing to build a resilient civic culture.

Collectively, these examples demonstrate that while many constitutions recognise education as essential for self-government, they do so through different mechanisms: justiciable rights, philosophical mandates, or unenforced principles. The crucial factor for democratic resilience, therefore, is not the mere presence of a constitutional clause, but its legal power and the political will to realise it.

Derek Black's argument is foundational: education is not merely a social service, but a constitutional necessity. Republican self-government requires citizens who are informed, thoughtful, and capable of exercising judgement. Education cultivates these capacities. Without it, self-government is impossible.

The four cases illustrate different approaches to constitutionalising education. South Africa and Kenya have adopted justiciable rights, enforceable through courts. Citizens can go to court to demand that the state fulfil its obligations. This creates accountability and pressure for implementation.

Bolivia has adopted a philosophical mandate, defining education in transformative terms. This approach signals a fundamental reorientation of the state's relationship with indigenous knowledge and power. But its effectiveness depends on political will and sustained effort.

The lesson for Botswana is clear: if education is to serve as a foundation for constitutional democracy, it must be more than an aspirational principle. It must be given legal force and backed by political will. It must be implemented effectively, reaching all citizens and building the capacities necessary for self-government.

12.5 CIVIC EDUCATION AS CONSTITUTIONAL MAINTENANCE

Vicki Jackson's notion of *constitutional maintenance* emphasises that constitutions require continuous institutional work to preserve legitimacy.

South Africa's post-apartheid initiatives, such as the Bill of Responsibilities, represented a significant state-driven effort at civic renewal. However, their lasting impact as a transformative national force remains contested, underscoring the challenge of translating a transitional campaign into enduring civic infrastructure.

The case of Bolivia presents a profound philosophical commitment to "intercultural education" within its constitutional framework. This commitment recognises the country's diverse Indigenous nations and seeks to integrate their distinct worldviews and languages into the national curriculum and governance structure. However, the journey from this constitutional principle to a universally "lived" plurinational reality is neither complete nor straightforward. Instead, it is an ongoing process that remains challenging and fraught with social tension, as the state navigates the practical implementation of radical inclusion while addressing historical hierarchies and persistent cultural conflicts.

Conversely, the Philippines exemplifies the consequence of systemic neglect, where the state's failure to build any continuous civic framework has left democratic norms vulnerable to erosion. This absence of a sustained pedagogical effort creates a vacuum, allowing democratic principles to be undermined by the forces of disinformation and populist appeals. The resulting lack of civic resilience provides a sharp contrast to cases where sustained, institutionalised civic education has successfully served as a corrective mechanism against democratic decay.

Together, these cases do not present a uniform blueprint. Still, rather a crucial lesson: for civic education to serve as a bulwark of constitutional democracy, it must be architected as permanent public infrastructure. Whether state-led or civil-society-driven, it requires a depth of integration that transcends symbolic campaigns or temporary interventions.

Vicki Jackson's concept of constitutional maintenance directs attention to the ongoing work of sustaining constitutional legitimacy. A constitution is not a one-time achievement; it requires continuous effort to preserve its meaning and authority. Civic education is a crucial form of constitutional maintenance.

South Africa's Bill of Responsibilities was an effort to embed constitutional values in civic life. By teaching citizens that rights come with responsibilities, it sought to cultivate the dispositions necessary for constitutional democracy. However, its impact remains contested, and the challenge of translating a transitional campaign into enduring infrastructure persists.

Bolivia's commitment to intercultural education is profound, but incomplete. The constitutional principle is clear, but implementation is challenging. Integrating indigenous worldviews into the national curriculum requires navigating historical hierarchies and persistent cultural conflicts. The journey from principle to practice is ongoing.

The Philippines demonstrates the consequences of neglect. Without sustained civic education, democratic norms have eroded. Disinformation and populism have filled the vacuum. The absence of civic infrastructure has left citizens vulnerable to manipulation.

The lesson is that civic education must be a permanent public infrastructure, not a temporary intervention. It must be integrated into schools, media, community organisations, and public life. It must be sustained over generations, not just activated during constitutional moments.

12.6 CIVIC EDUCATION AS DEMOCRATIC LEGITIMACY AND SOCIAL COHESION

Constitutions acquire legitimacy not only through ratification but through citizens' moral and epistemic engagement.

South Africa's Truth and Reconciliation Commission represented a profound national attempt to forge moral legitimacy by confronting the atrocities of apartheid. However, its ultimate success in securing universal social trust remains debated. Similarly, Kenya's civic forums sought to generate epistemic legitimacy by making the constitution's provisions accessible and understandable to the public.

Bolivia's integration of indigenous epistemologies into its education system is an ambitious, ongoing project to build cultural legitimacy and broaden the boundaries of the constitutional community. These efforts highlight the active role of civic pedagogy in nurturing a constitution's lived authority.

In contrast, the Philippines demonstrates the fragility of a narrow legitimacy base. While the 1987 Constitution achieved procedural legitimacy through its ratification, the state's subsequent failure to cultivate deeper moral and epistemic engagement among citizens has left its constitutional cohesion on a precarious foundation.

Collectively, these experiences suggest that robust constitutionalism is underpinned by legitimacy across multiple dimensions. Civic education serves as the primary mechanism for this construction. While not a guaranteed formula, this framework reveals that without sustained investment in the civic virtue and understanding of the people, a constitution's textual authority remains vulnerable to erosion.

Legitimacy has multiple dimensions. Procedural legitimacy comes from following the right processes. Moral legitimacy comes from the perceived justice of the constitutional order. Epistemic legitimacy comes from citizens' understanding of and engagement with the constitution. Cultural legitimacy comes from the constitution's resonance with the identities and values of the people.

Civic education contributes to all these dimensions. By teaching citizens about the constitution, it builds legitimacy. Engaging them in reflection on constitutional values, it builds moral legitimacy. By connecting constitutional principles to cultural identities, it builds cultural legitimacy. And by involving citizens in constitutional processes, it builds procedural legitimacy.

12.7 LESSONS FOR BOTSWANA

The comparative and theoretical analysis in this chapter yields several lessons for Botswana's constitutional review process.

First, civic education must begin early and continue throughout. It is not a preliminary step to be completed before the "real" work begins. It must run through every phase of the process, from preparation through adoption, and beyond. Citizens need ongoing opportunities to learn, ask questions, and deepen their understanding.

Second, civic education must be inclusive and accessible. It must reach all citizens, regardless of language, literacy, location, or disability. It must use multiple channels, from radio, television, print, digital, community forums, etc., to ensure a broad reach. It must be available in all major languages and accessible formats.

Third, civic education must be non-partisan and trustworthy. It must not be seen as propaganda for any particular party or interest. It should be delivered by trusted institutions, perhaps the independent review commission, in partnership with civil society organisations, educational institutions, and media. Its content should be factual and balanced, presenting different perspectives on constitutional issues.

Fourth, civic education must be both cognitive and affective. It must convey information: facts about the constitution, the process, and the issues. But it must also cultivate dispositions: commitment to democratic values, willingness to engage with others, capacity for deliberation. Both are essential.

Fifth, civic education must be connected to participation. Learning about the constitution should be linked to opportunities to engage with the process. Citizens should not just learn; they should also have chances to ask questions, share views, and influence outcomes. Civic education and public participation are two sides of the same coin.

Sixth, civic education must be sustained beyond the constitutional moment. The constitution will need ongoing maintenance. Citizens will need ongoing opportunities to learn about their rights and responsibilities, to engage with constitutional issues, and to defend constitutional values. Civic education should be built into the ongoing life of the constitutional order.

Seventh, civic education must attend to the information environment. In an era of social media, disinformation, and polarisation, civic education must equip citizens to navigate the information landscape critically. Media literacy is essential to informed citizenship.

12.8 CONCLUSION

Civic education is not a luxury or an add-on; it is essential to constitutional legitimacy and endurance. As the comparative cases demonstrate, sustained investment in civic education builds the capacities and dispositions that constitutional democracy requires. Neglect of civic education leaves constitutional orders vulnerable to decay, disinformation, and democratic backsliding.

For Botswana, the constitutional review process offers an opportunity to invest in civic education as both a means and an end. As a means, civic education will equip citizens to participate meaningfully in the review, ensuring that the resulting constitution reflects popular input and commands broad allegiance. As an end, civic education will build the civic capacities and dispositions that will sustain constitutional democracy for generations to come.

The challenge is significant. Botswana is a diverse country, with multiple languages, varied literacy levels, and communities spread across a large territory. Reaching all citizens with effective civic education will require resources, creativity, and sustained effort. But the payoff is immense: a citizenry that understands its constitution, that is committed to its principles, and that is capable of defending it against erosion and attack.

The chapters that follow trace the remaining phases of the constitutional review process. However, civic education is not confined to a single phase; it should infuse every stage, from preparation through adoption and beyond. The investment made in civic education during the review process will pay dividends long after the new constitution is adopted.

RECAP AND TRANSITION

Recap: This chapter has examined civic education as both a medium and a measure of democratic constitutionalism. It has drawn on the theoretical frameworks of Balkin (constitutional rot), McClain and Fleming (reflective patriotism), Black (education as a constitutional right), and Jackson (constitutional maintenance) to explain why civic education matters. It has examined comparative experiences from South Africa, Kenya, Bolivia, and the Philippines, identifying successes and failures. It has drawn lessons for Botswana: civic education must begin early and continue throughout; be inclusive and accessible; be non-partisan and trustworthy; be both cognitive and affective; be connected to participation; be sustained beyond the constitutional moment; and attend to the information environment.

Transition: Having established the foundational importance of civic education, the next chapter turns to the phase in which civic education bears fruit: public participation itself. Chapter Thirteen examines **National Consultation and Public Participation (Phase II)**. It explores how to design multi-channel submission systems, how to conduct grassroots consultations that reach all communities, and how to collect and synthesise public input transparently and systematically. Phase II is where the principles of inclusivity, accessibility and participation are put into practice, and where civic education enables citizens to engage meaningfully.

CHAPTER THIRTEEN

NATIONAL CONSULTATION AND PUBLIC PARTICIPATION

13.1 INTRODUCTION

National consultation and public participation are mechanisms that are designed to enable decision-makers to understand the real needs of society and to promote policies that are more appropriate, effective, and widely accepted. In designing the procedure for public participation, it is essential to take into account the potential challenges that such engagement may generate. These include the manipulation of the public by powerful interest groups, the ethnicisation of opinions, the risk of spontaneity and populism overshadowing informed debate, and the diminishing role of experts, all of which can make consensus-building more difficult.

An effective participation framework must therefore address the preparedness of the public, both psychologically and intellectually, to engage meaningfully in the process. This involves careful planning of the methods for soliciting views from the general public, as well as from organised and special-interest groups. Equally important are the procedures for the analysis, assessment, balancing, and incorporation of these views into the constitutional draft, to ensure that participation is both genuine and constructive.

Phase II represents the participatory core of constitution-making. The comparative record shows three main success factors:

1. A legally mandated, well-resourced, multi-channel intake system that balances digital access with robust physical outreach.
2. An extensive, well-planned grassroots programme that deliberately targets marginalised groups.

3. Rigorous, transparent data collection and synthesis (the "National Report") that feeds drafting.

The South African experience between 1994 and 1996, and Kenya between 2003 and 2010, provides the strongest operational models, demonstrating how broad engagement can be managed effectively. Namibia's Constituent Assembly functioned successfully within its historical context but was more elite-driven. By contrast, Zambia and Tanzania illustrate the risks associated with rushed, politicised, or underfunded public engagement. At the same time, Zimbabwe (2013) shows that even when formal mechanisms and a referendum are in place, trust, outreach, and perceived impartiality can remain weak.

This chapter examines the key components of Phase II: multi-channel public submission, grassroots consultations, and collection and synthesis, through comparative analysis, drawing lessons and best practices from different constitutional review processes. It concludes with recommendations for designing and implementing a participatory process that is genuine, inclusive and effective.

13.2 KEY COMPONENTS OF PHASE II

13.2.1 Multi-Channel Public Submission

One of the most compelling theoretical claims about popular participation relates to its impact on constitutionalism, that is, a constitution's capacity to constrain government. For citizens to effectively monitor and check government actions, they must have a clear understanding of what constitutes a breach of the limits of governmental power, enabling them to mobilise and act to prevent such violations. Multi-Channel Public Submission creates a platform for the public to interact with the constitutional-making or review process. This interaction is mainly performed to achieve three goals: to provide public services, improve managerial effect, and promote democracy.

An essential reason why multi-channel public submission should be considered was pointed out by Elster: that a constitution that is produced in more democratic processes will tend to be more democratic. A central dimension on which constitution-making processes differ is the degree of public participation. Since a constitution represents the highest form of law and provides the ultimate rule of recognition for all other law-making processes, it demands the highest level of legitimacy in democratic theory. Emphasising public participation allows us to appreciate the complexity and dynamics of constitution-making, highlighting the diverse interests and groups that often seek, or wish, to be involved in shaping the fundamental law. One of the important ways to maintain public participation is through Multi-Channel Public Submission.

The concept of multi-channel submission recognises that different citizens prefer different modes of engagement. Some are comfortable with digital platforms, others prefer to submit written memoranda, and still others want to participate through sectoral hearings where they can engage directly with experts and decision-makers. A well-designed system offers all these options, maximising accessibility and inclusion.

13.2.1.1 Digital Platforms

Multi-Channel Public Submission will cover both digital platforms, physical submissions, and sectoral hearings. To facilitate broad public participation, multiple channels should be established for collecting input. Digital platforms, such as a dedicated website and social media channels, can be used for online submissions, surveys, and discussion forums. Therefore, creating a dedicated website and social media channels for online submissions, surveys, and discussion forums will create an avenue for public participation where individuals can contribute their voices.

Digital platforms offer significant advantages. They can reach large numbers of people quickly and cheaply. They allow citizens to participate at their convenience, without needing to travel to physical venues.

They can include interactive features—surveys, forums, live chats—that enhance engagement. They can be updated continuously as the process evolves.

But digital platforms also have limitations. They require internet access, which is not universal. They may exclude older citizens, rural communities, and those with limited digital literacy. They can be vulnerable to manipulation by organised campaigns or automated bots. They cannot replicate the depth of face-to-face dialogue.

For these reasons, digital platforms should be seen as one channel among many, not as a replacement for other forms of engagement. They are most effective when integrated with physical submissions and sectoral hearings, creating a comprehensive multi-channel system.

13.2.1.2 Physical Submissions

Physical submission points should be established in post offices, government buildings, and libraries to receive written memoranda. This approach allows ordinary citizens and civil society organisations to actively participate in the drafting process by submitting their proposals for constitutional reform, thereby broadening engagement and ensuring that diverse perspectives are considered.

The submission of reform proposals has been an integral part of the drafting process in recent constitution-making episodes in sub-Saharan Africa, such as South Africa (1993–1996) and Kenya (2009–2010). These submission processes are intended to encourage citizens to take a proactive role in expressing their needs and preferences regarding the new constitution. However, the extent to which these submissions influence the outcome often remains a subject of debate and controversy. Nonetheless, particularly in competitive political environments, referenda can exert a significant influence on the outcome of the constitution-making process.

Physical submission points provide an accessible option for those without internet access. By locating them in familiar, trusted places—post offices, government buildings, libraries—the process becomes more approachable. Citizens can submit written memoranda in their own words, at their own pace, without needing to navigate digital interfaces.

The experience of South Africa and Kenya demonstrates that physical submissions can generate significant participation. In South Africa, over two million submissions were received, many through physical collection points. This volume of input created a rich evidence base for drafting, though it also required substantial analytical capacity to process.

13.2.1.3 Sectoral Hearings

In addition to Multi-Channel Public Submission through digital platforms and physical submissions, sectoral hearings should be held on key thematic issues, such as governance structures, human rights, land ownership, and natural resources, which will bring experts and relevant interest groups together to provide informed input.

These mechanisms are designed to enhance the democratic legitimacy of the constitution-making process by allowing ordinary citizens to express their preferences and, in some cases, to provide actual consent to the changes proposed by their representatives. From this perspective, a notable example of meaningful and consequential participation is the extensive programme of public education and consultation conducted in South Africa between February 1995 and February 1996, before the drafting of the final constitutional text.

Sectoral hearings serve a different purpose from general submissions. They bring together experts and interest groups with specialised knowledge to provide informed input on specific issues. A hearing on land ownership, for example, might include representatives of farmers' organisations, traditional leaders, land rights advocates, academic experts, and government officials. Their collective expertise can illuminate complex issues and inform drafting.

Sectoral hearings also enhance legitimacy by demonstrating that the process takes the concerns of specific communities and interests. When farmers see that their representatives have been heard on land issues, they are more likely to accept the eventual constitutional provisions.

National consultation and participation may also require the involvement of the public in selecting the individuals who will draft or deliberate on various aspects of the constitution, ensuring that the process reflects broad societal representation and legitimacy. One of the most compelling theoretical arguments for popular participation relates to its impact on constitutionalism, specifically, a constitution's capacity to constrain governmental power. For citizens to effectively monitor and check government actions, they must clearly understand what constitutes a breach of the limits of authority, enabling them to mobilise and prevent such violations.

Public participation is one of the emerging guiding principles in constitution-making. It is essential for embedding broad participatory mechanisms into the process and for enhancing the likelihood that the resulting constitution will enjoy a high degree of popular legitimacy.

Participation thus legitimates and constrains, substituting inclusive processes for consent to make effective government possible. They include preparing the public to participate through civic education and public information campaigns, as well as consulting the public on issues such as whether a process should take place (and how) and what should be in the constitution itself. In fact, a common approach may involve the public in selecting the individuals who will draft or deliberate on various aspects of the constitution, ensuring that the process reflects broad societal representation and legitimacy.

13.2.1.4 Comparative Analysis of the Case Studies

The analysis of the selected case studies reveals that public input is collected through digital platforms, physical submission points, and sectoral hearings to ensure broad access and inclusivity. South Africa, between 1994 and 1996, exemplifies a large-scale, well-managed approach, receiving over two million submissions via official collection points, mail, and structured public hearings, with extensive media and community liaison support. The process provided legitimacy and a rich evidence base for drafting, though managing volume and varying submission quality required substantial analytical capacity.

South Africa's experience demonstrates what is possible with adequate resources and planning. The multi-channel system reached millions of citizens, generating a wealth of input that informed the drafting process. The challenge of managing such volume was real, but it was met through systematic coding and analysis.

The Kenyan constitutional review process of 2010 combined multiple channels for public engagement. Online platforms allowed citizens to submit views and monitor the process, while thousands of written memoranda were submitted through physical collection centres across the country. Sectoral hearings were held with key constituencies, including women, youth, business groups, pastoralist communities, and persons with disabilities. The process was anchored in the Constitution of Kenya Review Act, which legally mandated broad public participation and established binding procedural standards.

Kenya's experience illustrates the value of a legally mandated framework. The Constitution of Kenya Review Act did not leave participation to discretion; it required it. This legal mandate ensured that participation was not sacrificed to expediency and that procedures were followed consistently.

Namibia's 1990 Constituent Assembly relied more on elite-driven submissions, with fewer grassroots mechanisms, achieving efficient drafting but limited mass participation. Kenya (2003–2010) combined statutory authority, multi-channel intake, and expert management through the Committee of Experts, producing public synthesis reports that informed parliamentary debate and the referendum. In contrast, Zambia, Tanzania, and Zimbabwe faced challenges including ad hoc or executive-dominated collection, limited outreach, and political interference, resulting in weaker legitimacy and incomplete public input.

The negative examples reinforce the importance of the success factors identified earlier. Where collection was ad hoc or executive-dominated, where outreach was limited, and where political interference was present, legitimacy suffered. The process may have produced a constitution, but it did not produce ownership.

13.2.2 Grassroots Consultations

In the participatory process, the purpose is to engage with individuals and groups with differing interests so that they can advance those interests. The Commission (whether an ICRC, Committee of Experts, or Constitutional Review Commission) is typically a smaller, technically oriented body mandated to collect public views, analyse and synthesise those inputs, and prepare the draft constitutional text.

The ICRC travels to every region and district to hold town hall meetings, public hearings, and focus group discussions. The importance of broad popular participation in constitution-making has varied across countries. Still, in contexts where civic groups, unions, media outlets, and political parties are few, weakly established, or have limited reach, it becomes even more essential to create special arrangements for the direct involvement of citizens. Such mechanisms help convey and gather information, strengthen public understanding of constitutional issues, and cultivate a culture of constitutionalism. Public participation is understood to strengthen national unity by ensuring that the constitution-making process is inclusive and reflective of a country's religious, cultural, and linguistic diversity. An open and participatory process helps resolve national differences and strike an appropriate balance between shared national identity and the distinct values of regional or cultural communities.

Grassroots consultations are the most intensive form of public participation. They involve face-to-face engagement between commission members and citizens in communities across the country. They allow for deep dialogue where citizens can ask questions, explore issues, and articulate their views in their own words.

The logistical challenges are significant. Travelling to every district requires resources and planning. Holding meetings in multiple languages requires interpreters and translated materials. Reaching remote communities requires creativity and persistence. But the payoff is immense: citizens feel heard, and the commission gains a deep understanding of local realities and concerns.

Grassroots Consultations are crucial for inclusivity (including gender equity) and representation as it adopts targeted methods to reach specific groups, which include Women-Only Forums to discuss gender-specific issues without intimidation. An inclusive process will attempt to draw in all key stakeholders to the constitutional negotiations. Special efforts will be made to reach out to marginalised segments of society, such as the disabled, women, youth, indigenous populations, and the poorest of the poor.

Targeted methods are essential for reaching groups that might otherwise be excluded. Women may be hesitant to speak in mixed forums, particularly on sensitive issues. Women-only forums create safe spaces where they can articulate their views without intimidation. Youth may be more comfortable in forums designed for them, using language and formats that resonate. Persons with disabilities need venues that are physically accessible and materials in accessible formats.

Some recent constitutional processes have deliberately undertaken special measures to ensure that women are represented by at least 25 per cent in constitution-making bodies, and that they participate more fully during each stage of the process (e.g., Afghanistan in 2004). Ensuring women's full participation in the constitution-making process requires deliberate measures across all stages. This includes embedding gender-inclusive rules of procedure within the relevant institutions; designing civic education and public consultation programmes that specifically reach and empower women; ensuring that women are adequately represented as staff members and leaders within administrative and management bodies; and supporting their active involvement in civil society through roles such as lobbying, advocacy, and monitoring the work of constitution-makers.

Grassroots Consultations also encourage activities such as youth dialogues in universities and community centres. Meetings with Indigenous and Traditional Leaders in their communities, including accessible venues for persons with disabilities. Public participation is understood to strengthen national unity by ensuring that the constitution-making process is inclusive and reflective of a country's religious, cultural and linguistic diversity. An open and participatory process helps resolve national differences and strike an appropriate balance between shared national identity and the distinct values of regional or cultural communities.

As a result, the careful analysis of public views becomes especially important when constitution-making institutions are required to incorporate the people's recommendations. In such contexts, public inputs are not merely symbolic; they form a substantive part of the constitution-building process and must, therefore, be assessed systematically, transparently, and with due regard to their relevance and implications.

13.2.2.1 Extensive Public Participation

South Africa is widely celebrated as a case where public participation was extensive, and the resulting 1996 Constitution reflects this engagement through its strong emphasis on rights, inclusion, accountability, and broad democratic legitimacy. The South African constitutional review process (1994–1996) featured extensive public engagement, including door-to-door campaigns, town hall meetings, and rural consultations. Meetings were conducted in multiple languages, with interpreters provided to ensure accessibility. This approach successfully included rural, poor, and marginalised communities, giving them a voice in shaping the constitution.

However, the process was resource-intensive and presented significant logistical challenges in reaching remote areas.

South Africa's experience demonstrates both the potential and the challenges of extensive grassroots engagement. The process reached communities that had never before been consulted on constitutional matters. Meetings were conducted in multiple languages, with interpreters ensuring accessibility. The result was a constitution that reflected the input of millions of ordinary citizens.

But the challenges were real. The process was resource-intensive, requiring substantial funding and logistical capacity. Reaching remote areas was difficult. Managing the volume of input required sophisticated systems. These challenges were met, but they could not be ignored.

When the Kenyan constitutional review process began at the end of 2000, there was broad agreement on a design that featured a central role for experts and extensive popular participation. However, as the implications of constitution-making, both in terms of substantive reforms and the potential empowerment of citizens, became apparent, this consensus broke down, with politicians attempting to exclude other actors from decision-making. By mid-2004, political leaders had assumed control of the process, and by 2008, the review was firmly dominated by the political class.

Kenya's experience illustrates the fragility of participatory consensus. When the process began, there was broad agreement on the importance of popular participation. But as the stakes became clear, politicians moved to assert control. The lesson is that participation cannot be taken for granted; it must be defended throughout the process.

The Namibian process relied primarily on political parties and elite actors, with very limited grassroots civic engagement. While this approach allowed for a relatively quick drafting process, it did little to foster long-term legitimacy through broad public involvement.

Namibia's experience represents the opposite end of the spectrum: elite-driven, efficient, but with limited popular engagement. The constitution was adopted relatively quickly and has functioned adequately, but it lacks the deep popular ownership that participatory processes can generate.

Zambia attempted public consultations, but these were poorly documented and often lacked effective facilitation. Many rural areas were not reached, undermining the inclusivity of the process. While the intentions behind the consultations were commendable, inconsistent execution weakened both their effectiveness and credibility.

Zambia's experience shows that good intentions are not enough. Consultations must be well-planned, well-documented and effectively facilitated. They must reach all areas, not just those that are easily accessible. Inconsistent execution can undermine credibility and waste resources.

Tanzania achieved one of the most comprehensive grassroots outreach efforts in Africa. The Constitutional Review Commission visited every district and village and organised women-only and youth-only forums to encourage participation. Despite the thoroughness of the engagement, political actors often ignored the results, limiting the practical impact of citizen input.

Tanzania's experience raises a different concern: what happens when thorough engagement is followed by political disregard? The Commission did its job, reaching every district and village, organising targeted forums. But when the results were presented, political actors ignored them. Participation without impact breeds cynicism.

Zimbabwe also held national consultations, but in many rural areas, the environment was characterised by intimidation. Some citizens were coerced either to speak in favour of official positions or to remain silent. While the process reached a wide geographic area, the lack of a free and fair environment undermined the legitimacy and authenticity of participation.

Zimbabwe's experience illustrates the most serious failure: participation in an unfree environment. When citizens are coerced or intimidated, their "input" is meaningless. The process may appear participatory, but it is actually a tool of domination.

13.2.3 Collection and Synthesis

Collection and Synthesis entail a process of systematic collection of all data from every channel (which includes notes from meetings, online submissions, and survey results). The ICRC technical team then synthesises this information into a "National Report of Public Views," which identifies key themes, points of consensus, and contentious issues. This report is subsequently shared widely with the population to ensure transparency and inform further deliberation.

Collection and synthesis are the bridge between participation and drafting. They transform raw input (millions of submissions, thousands of meeting notes, and countless survey responses) into structured information that can guide constitutional design. This is a technical task, but it is also a political one. How input is categorised, what themes are identified, and how consensus and divergence are characterised, all shape the outcome.

Transparency can significantly influence how self-interest is expressed in constitution-making processes. When procedures, decisions, and data are openly accessible, actors are less able to pursue narrow or hidden agendas without scrutiny. Open processes create accountability, reduce opportunities for manipulation and can encourage participants to align their actions with broader public expectations, rather than purely personal or partisan gain.

The South African experience, in which public input and elite bargaining were followed by a certification process by the constitutional court, provides another innovative model. The precise need for transparency and secrecy in negotiation may depend on particular contextual circumstances. South Africa produced a Public Participation Report in which submissions were categorised by theme and published transparently. Its strength lay in the academic-level rigour, though the sheer volume of inputs made processing difficult.

South Africa's approach set a high standard. Submissions were categorised by theme, analysed systematically and published transparently. The resulting report provided a clear picture of public views, which then informed drafting. The challenge was managing the sheer volume of input, which required substantial analytical capacity.

Namibia relied primarily on elite negotiations and SWAPO's position, with no large-scale synthesis report. This approach was efficient but lacked genuine public participation.

Kenya implemented structured thematic analysis, documenting views in CRC reports, county summaries, and final national reports. This represented the best synthesis model, though politicians, at times, tried to influence outcomes.

Zambia faced poor archiving and confusion between technical experts and politicians, regarding public input. The result was a lack of rigour and diminished public trust.

Tanzania's CRC produced a massive, highly rigorous report detailing public preferences. Its strength was in the quality of synthesis, but the government largely ignored the findings.

Zimbabwe's COPAC compiled a report, but political parties frequently disputed the findings. The interpretation of citizens' inputs was heavily politicised, undermining credibility.

As Brandt et al inform us:

"A transparent process enables the public, the media, and civil society to participate by keeping them informed about how the process will be conducted, the modes of appointment and election of their representatives, the adoption process, their role in the process, and providing feedback about the results of public consultations. Transparency also involves providing for media access at appropriate times."

As a result, understanding the role of a constitution is essential for designing the process of its creation, as it shapes the objectives, structures, and mechanisms of participation, ensuring that the resulting document effectively guides governance, protects rights, and maintains legitimacy.

13.3 CONCLUDING REMARKS

Constitution-making is a complex, political and inherently participatory process. The experience from South Africa and Kenya demonstrates the effectiveness of legally mandated public participation, complemented by dedicated and well-funded civic education campaigns. The transparent publication of submissions, the presence of independent commissions with strong credibility, and consultations conducted across multiple platforms (both digital and grassroots), fostered legitimacy and broad ownership. In Tanzania, the deep grassroots listening sessions across villages provided valuable insights into local needs. At the same time, Namibia showed that efficiency and clear political commitment can help advance the process, though more structured public input was needed to strengthen legitimacy.

Conversely, experiences in Zambia highlight the pitfalls of weak documentation, lack of transparency, and inconsistent national coverage, which undermine credibility. In Tanzania, the failure of the government to act on public input diminished trust in the process. Zimbabwe illustrates the dangers of intimidation, political interference, and the politicised interpretation of public views, which can erode the legitimacy of the constitutional outcome.

13.4 RECOMMENDATIONS FOR NATIONAL CONSULTATION AND PUBLIC PARTICIPATION (PHASE II)

Based on comparative analysis, the following steps are recommended to ensure broad, inclusive and credible public engagement:

13.4.1 Build Multi-Channel Public Submission

A multi-channel public submissions system should be implemented, combining digital platforms (including a dedicated website, WhatsApp, and SMS-based tools, which adapt to the modern model) with physical submission points at post offices and community centres, drawing from South Africa's approach.

13.4.2 Fund a Nationwide Grassroots Consultation Programme

One of the main challenges to the grassroots consultation programme is funding. A nationwide grassroots consultation programme must be funded and executed, with district-by-district town halls, targeted forums for women and youth, and venues accessible to persons with disabilities, reflecting lessons from Kenya and Tanzania.

The consultation process must be protected from political interference. Meetings should be secured, and no political party should dominate messaging, learning from the experiences of Zimbabwe.

13.4.3 Ensure Systematic Collection and Transparent Synthesis

Finally, all submissions should be published, and a National Report of Public Views should be produced. This report should provide a transparent, systematic and thematic analysis of public input, as demonstrated effectively in South Africa and Kenya.

RECAP AND TRANSITION

Recap: This chapter has examined Phase II of constitutional review: national consultation and public participation. It has explored three key components: multi-channel public submission (digital platforms, physical submissions and sectoral hearings); grassroots consultations (town hall meetings, public hearings, focus group discussions and targeted methods for reaching marginalised groups); and collection and synthesis (systematic data collection, thematic analysis and transparent reporting). It has drawn on comparative experience from South Africa, Kenya, Namibia, Zambia, Tanzania and Zimbabwe to identify best practices and common pitfalls. It has concluded with recommendations: build a multi-channel public submission system; fund a nationwide grassroots consultation programme protected from political interference; and ensure systematic collection and transparent synthesis of all input.

Transition: Having gathered public input through extensive consultation, the next chapter turns to the phase in which that input is analysed and translated into constitutional language. Chapter Fourteen examines **Phase III: Analysis, Drafting, and Further Public Engagement**. It explores how to code and cluster submissions, how to identify convergences and divergences, how to draft revision proposals, and how to engage the public in testing and refining drafts. This phase is the bridge between consultation and decision-making, ensuring that public voices are not lost in translation.

Chapter Fourteen

PHASE THREE – ANALYSIS, DRAFTING AND FURTHER PUBLIC ENGAGEMENT

14.1 INTRODUCTION

Phase III of the Constitutional Review Process, which involves the analysis of submissions, clustering of themes, and drafting of proposals, is pivotal. International best practice demonstrates that this stage must combine technical rigour with inclusive public engagement. Without it, reforms risk being elite-driven; with it, they can embody the aspirations of the people.

Phase III transforms raw citizen input into structured constitutional options. It requires thematic clustering, identification of convergences and divergences, and the drafting of models for revision. Comparative experiences show that this stage is the bridge between consultation and decision-making, ensuring that public voices are not lost in translation.

The preceding phases – Foundation and Preparation (Phase I), Civic Education, and National Consultation and Public Participation (Phase II) – have laid the groundwork. The Commission has been established, the public has been educated and consulted, and millions of submissions have been received. Now begins the painstaking work of making sense of it all.

Phase III is where the voice of the people is translated into the language of constitutional law. It is a technical task, requiring rigorous methodology and analytical skill. But it is also a deeply political task, requiring judgement about what the people have said and what it means for the constitutional text. Getting it right is essential to maintaining the legitimacy that participation has generated.

14.2 PHASE 3: ANALYTICAL FOUNDATIONS

The analytical work begins with coding submissions into categories such as governance, rights, decentralisation, and accountability. This process must be transparent and methodologically sound. South Africa's Constitutional Assembly in 1996 employed expert teams to code over two million submissions, ensuring that every voice was represented. Kenya's Committee of Experts in 2010 similarly categorised inputs into thematic areas, which guided the drafting process. Botswana must adopt comparable rigour to ensure legitimacy.

Coding is the process of categorising submissions by theme. A submission about presidential powers would be coded under "governance," and perhaps more specifically under "executive." A submission about women's rights would be coded under "rights" and "gender." A submission about local government would be coded under "decentralisation."

The coding scheme must be designed before analysis begins. It should be comprehensive enough to capture all the issues raised, but not so detailed that it becomes unwieldy. It should be tested on a sample of submissions and refined as needed, and it should be applied consistently by all coders, which requires training and supervision.

South Africa's experience demonstrates what is possible. Expert teams coded over two million submissions, a monumental task. But the effort paid off: the resulting analysis ensured that every voice was represented, that no submission was lost in the shuffle. Kenya's Committee of Experts similarly categorised inputs by theme, producing a structured picture of public views that guided drafting.

14.3 CLUSTERING THEMES AND IDENTIFYING DIVERGENCES

Clustering themes involves grouping similar submissions to identify dominant concerns. Divergences must also be documented, as minority positions often highlight critical issues. Bolivia's 2009 process illustrates this: indigenous autonomy was a minority demand initially, but became central to the final constitution. Botswana's Commission must therefore balance majority views with minority protections, ensuring inclusivity.

Clustering is the process of grouping coded submissions to identify patterns. How many submissions addressed land reform? What were the main concerns raised? Were there regional variations in views? Clustering answers these questions, revealing the contours of public opinion.

But clustering must not obscure divergence. Minority views matter, both substantively and strategically. Substantively, they may highlight issues that the majority has overlooked but that are critical for certain communities. Strategically, excluding minority views can breed resentment and undermine the legitimacy of the final constitution.

Bolivia's experience is instructive. Indigenous autonomy was initially a minority demand, pressed by communities that had long been marginalised. But through sustained advocacy and deliberation, it became central to the final constitution. The 2009 Constitution recognises Bolivia as a plurinational state and grants significant autonomy to indigenous communities. This outcome would have been impossible if minority views had been dismissed.

Botswana's Commission must therefore attend to both convergence and divergence. It must identify where the people agree, building consensus around those issues. But, it must also document where they disagree, ensuring that minority perspectives are not lost, and that contentious issues receive the attention they deserve.

14.4 DRAFTING REVISION PROPOSALS

Once themes are clustered, draft proposals or models must be generated. These can take the form of incremental amendments or comprehensive revisions. South Africa's process produced successive working drafts, each tested against public opinion. Kenya's Committee of Experts released many drafts, refining them through feedback. Botswana should consider multiple models, for example, one emphasising incremental reform and another proposing comprehensive restructuring, to allow public debate on alternatives.

Drafting is where analysis becomes text. The clustered themes and identified issues must be translated into constitutional language. This requires both technical expertise and substantive judgement.

The form of proposals can vary. Incremental amendments propose changes to specific provisions while leaving the overall structure intact. Comprehensive revisions propose a new constitutional framework, potentially reimagining the entire order. Each approach has advantages and disadvantages, and different stakeholders may prefer different approaches.

South Africa's iterative process offers a model. Successive working drafts were produced, each tested against public opinion. This allowed for continuous refinement, with each draft incorporating feedback on the previous one. It also kept the public engaged throughout the drafting phase, as citizens could see how their input was being used.

Kenya's Committee of Experts similarly released multiple drafts, refining them through feedback. This iterative approach builds legitimacy by demonstrating responsiveness. Citizens see that their views matter, that the process is not just going through the motions.

Botswana should consider presenting multiple models for public debate. One model might emphasise incremental reform, proposing targeted amendments to address specific issues. Another might propose comprehensive restructuring, reimagining the constitutional order for the twenty-first century. Presenting alternatives would allow citizens to debate not just specific provisions, but fundamental choices about the direction of reform.

14.5 PUBLIC ENGAGEMENT IN PHASE 3

Public engagement is essential at this stage. Draft proposals must be tested through town halls, surveys, and digital platforms. South Africa's Constitutional Assembly published drafts widely, inviting public comment. Kenya's process involved civic education campaigns to explain proposals before feedback was solicited. Bolivia's Constituent Assembly held regional forums to debate draft texts. Botswana must similarly ensure that citizens understand proposals before being asked to respond.

Public engagement does not end with Phase II. It continues through Phase III, as draft proposals are developed and refined. This is not a departure from the participatory model, but a deepening of it. Citizens are not just consulted at the front end; they are engaged throughout as proposals take shape.

South Africa's approach was to publish drafts widely and invite public comment. This allowed citizens to see how their input had been used and to respond to the emerging text. It also created opportunities for civil society organisations to analyse drafts and advocate for changes.

Kenya's process involved civic education campaigns to explain proposals before feedback was solicited. This ensured that citizens understood what they were responding to, that their feedback was informed rather than superficial.

Bolivia's Constituent Assembly held regional forums to debate draft texts. These forums allowed for deep engagement, with citizens discussing proposals in detail and suggesting refinements.

For Botswana, the lesson is clear: public engagement must continue through Phase III. Draft proposals should be published and explained. Citizens should have opportunities to respond, through town halls, surveys, and digital platforms. Their feedback should be collected, analysed, and used to refine subsequent drafts.

14.6 INTERNATIONAL BEST PRACTICES: TRANSPARENCY

Transparency is a cornerstone of legitimacy. Publishing draft proposals, explaining methodologies, and documenting how submissions are analysed builds trust. South Africa's process was lauded for its openness, with all drafts and submissions made publicly available. Kenya's Committee of Experts also emphasised transparency, publishing reports and rationales for decisions. Botswana should adopt similar practices to avoid perceptions of secrecy.

Transparency in Phase III means making visible the work of analysis and drafting. It means publishing the coding scheme and explaining how submissions were categorised. It means releasing the National Report of Public Views, documenting what the people said. It means publishing draft proposals and explaining how they respond to public input. It means providing rationales for decisions, showing why certain proposals were included and others rejected.

South Africa set a high standard. All drafts and submissions were made publicly available. Citizens could see exactly what was being proposed and how their input had been used.

Kenya's Committee of Experts similarly emphasised transparency. Reports were published, rationales were provided, and decisions were explained. This openness helped maintain public confidence, even when the process became contentious.

For Botswana, adopting similar practices is essential. Secrecy breeds suspicion, transparency builds trust. The process must be open to public scrutiny at every stage.

14.7 INTERNATIONAL BEST PRACTICES: INCLUSIVITY

Inclusivity requires deliberate efforts to engage marginalised groups. Women, youth, rural communities, and minorities must see their voices reflected. Bolivia's process was notable for incorporating indigenous perspectives, reshaping the constitution around autonomy and resource governance. Botswana must ensure that inclusivity is not symbolic but substantive, with mechanisms to guarantee representation in analysis and drafting.

Inclusivity in Phase III means ensuring that marginalised groups are not just consulted, but actually reflected in the analysis and drafting. Their submissions must be coded and clustered alongside others. Their concerns must be identified and addressed. Their perspectives must shape the draft proposals.

Bolivia's experience is exemplary. Indigenous perspectives were not just solicited; they reshaped the entire constitutional framework. The 2009 Constitution recognises Bolivia as a plurinational state, grants autonomy to indigenous communities, and protects indigenous customary law. This transformation would have been impossible without substantive inclusivity; without ensuring that indigenous voices were not just heard but heeded.

For Botswana, the challenge is to ensure that inclusivity is substantive, not symbolic. This means going beyond counting the number of submissions from marginalised groups. It means analysing those submissions carefully, identifying the concerns they raise, and ensuring that those concerns are addressed in draft proposals. It may require targeted outreach during Phase III, seeking feedback from marginalised groups on draft provisions that affect them.

14.8 INTERNATIONAL BEST PRACTICES: ITERATIVE DRAFTING

It seems to me that producing successive versions of proposals and refining them through feedback is critical. South Africa's process involved multiple drafts, each tested against public opinion. Kenya's Committee of Experts adopted a similar iterative approach. Botswana should plan for at least two rounds of draft proposals, allowing for refinement and consensus-building.

Iterative drafting recognises that the first draft is rarely the best. It is a starting point, a proposal to be tested and refined. By releasing successive versions, the Commission demonstrates responsiveness and builds ownership. Each round of feedback allows citizens to see how their input has been used and to engage with the evolving text.

South Africa's multiple drafts were each tested against public opinion. This allowed for continuous refinement, with each iteration incorporating feedback on the previous one. It also kept the public engaged throughout the drafting phase, as citizens could track the evolution of the text.

Kenya's Committee of Experts adopted a similar approach, releasing multiple drafts and refining them through feedback. This iterative process helped build consensus, as stakeholders could see their concerns being addressed.

Botswana should plan for at least two rounds of draft proposals. The first round would present initial proposals based on analysis of public input. Public feedback would be collected and analysed. The second round would present refined proposals, incorporating that feedback. Further rounds could be added if needed. This iterative approach builds legitimacy and ownership.

14.9 CHALLENGES AND RISKS

Phase III is not without risks.

- **Political capture:** Elites may dominate the process.
- **Public fatigue:** Citizens may disengage if consultations are repetitive.
- **Managing divergences:** Deep disagreements may stall progress.

Bolivia's process faced significant polarisation, with debates over autonomy nearly derailing the assembly. Botswana must anticipate such risks and design safeguards.

Political capture is a persistent risk. Elites (political parties, powerful interest groups, wealthy individuals) may seek to dominate the process, ensuring that their voices drown out others. This is particularly dangerous in Phase III, where analysis and drafting occur away from public view. Safeguards include transparency (making the process visible), inclusivity (ensuring diverse participation), and independent oversight (monitoring for undue influence).

Public fatigue is another risk. Citizens who have participated in Phase II may feel that their work is done. They may not engage with Phase III, missing opportunities to shape draft proposals. This risk can be mitigated by communicating clearly about the ongoing nature of the process, by making engagement in Phase III accessible and meaningful, and by demonstrating responsiveness to feedback.

Managing divergences is perhaps the greatest challenge. Deep disagreements may emerge that cannot be easily resolved. Bolivia's process faced significant polarisation over autonomy, with debates nearly derailing the assembly. Such disagreements must be managed carefully, through dialogue, mediation, and sometimes compromise. The goal is not to eliminate divergence (that would be impossible and undesirable) but to find ways of accommodating it within the constitutional framework.

14.10 SAFEGUARDS FOR BOTSWANA

Safeguards include independent facilitation, expert support, and clear communication strategies. South Africa's Constitutional Assembly benefited from independent experts who ensured technical soundness. Kenya's Committee of Experts was insulated from political interference. Botswana should similarly empower its Commission with independence and resources.

Independent facilitation means that the process is managed by actors who are neutral and trusted. This may include the Commission itself, if it has maintained its independence. It may include external facilitators brought in to manage contentious meetings. The key is that no party to the process should control the facilitation.

Expert support means that the Commission has access to the technical expertise it needs. Constitutional drafting is complex; it requires knowledge of comparative law, constitutional design, and legal language. South Africa's Constitutional Assembly benefited from independent experts who ensured technical soundness. Kenya's Committee of Experts was itself composed of experts, insulated from political interference.

Clear communication strategies mean that the public is kept informed throughout Phase III. They know what is happening, why, and how they can engage. They understand the timeline and the process. They receive feedback on how their input has been used. This communication maintains engagement and builds trust.

14.11 COMMUNICATION STRATEGIES

Effective communication ensures that citizens understand proposals. Civic education campaigns, media partnerships and digital platforms can disseminate information widely. Kenya's 2010 process invested heavily in civic education, which was critical to public engagement. Botswana must prioritise communication to avoid alienation.

Communication in Phase III has several objectives. First, it must inform citizens about draft proposals. What do they contain? Why were they chosen? How do they respond to public input? Second, it must invite feedback. How can citizens comment on drafts? What is the process for submitting views? When will feedback be considered? Third, it must provide updates. What changes have been made in response to feedback? What issues remain contentious? What happens next?

Kenya's experience demonstrates the value of sustained communication. Civic education campaigns ran throughout the process, keeping citizens informed and engaged. Media partnerships amplified key messages. Digital platforms provided accessible information.

Botswana must prioritise communication. Without it, citizens may become alienated from the process. They may not understand what is happening or why. They may not know how to engage. They may lose trust. Communication is not an add-on; it is essential to legitimacy.

14.12 COMPARATIVE CASE STUDY: SOUTH AFRICA

South Africa's 1996 process exemplifies best practice. Over two million submissions were analysed, clustered, and transformed into drafts. Transparency, inclusivity and iterative drafting ensured legitimacy. The final constitution is widely regarded as one of the most progressive globally, reflecting the voices of citizens.

South Africa's success was not accidental. It resulted from careful design and sustained effort. The analysis of over two million submissions was a monumental task, but it was done systematically and transparently. The clustering of themes revealed the contours of public opinion. The iterative drafting process ensured that drafts were tested and refined. The result is a constitution that is widely admired and deeply owned.

14.13 COMPARATIVE CASE STUDY: KENYA

Kenya's 2010 process emphasised coming up with several drafts and civic education. Drafts were circulated widely, critiqued and refined. Inclusivity was prioritised, with deliberate efforts to engage marginalised groups. The final constitution introduced significant reforms, including devolution and expanded rights.

Kenya's process demonstrates the value of multiple drafts and sustained civic education. Drafts were not kept secret; they were circulated widely for critique and refinement. Inclusivity was not just rhetoric; deliberate efforts were made to engage marginalised groups. The resulting constitution introduced transformative reforms, including devolution, which have reshaped Kenyan governance.

14.14 COMPARATIVE CASE STUDY: BOLIVIA

Bolivia's 2009 process highlighted the importance of minority voices. Indigenous autonomy, initially a minority demand, became central to the constitution. The process was contentious, but ultimately produced a text that reflected Bolivia's diverse identities. Botswana can learn from Bolivia's emphasis on inclusivity and minority protections.

Bolivia's experience is particularly instructive for Botswana. Both countries have diverse populations with historically marginalised groups. In Bolivia, indigenous voices were not just heard but heeded. Their demands for autonomy and recognition reshaped the constitutional framework. The process was contentious; debates over autonomy nearly derailed the assembly, but the outcome was a constitution that reflects the nation's diversity.

Botswana can learn from Bolivia's emphasis on inclusivity and minority protections. It must ensure that marginalised groups are not just consulted, but actually reflected in the final constitution. It must be willing to engage with contentious issues, to deliberate through disagreement, and to find ways of accommodating diversity within the constitutional framework.

14.15 RECOMMENDATIONS FOR BOTSWANA

Botswana should:

- Adopt transparent methodologies.
- Ensure inclusivity through deliberate outreach.
- Employ iterative drafting.
- Safeguard independence of the Commission.
- Invest in civic education and communication.

These measures will align Botswana's process with international best practice.

Adopt transparent methodologies. The coding scheme should be published. The clustering process should be explained. The National Report of Public Views should be made public. Draft proposals should be released with explanations of how they respond to public input. Rationales for decisions should be provided.

Ensure inclusivity through deliberate outreach. Marginalised groups must be actively engaged in Phase III. Their feedback on draft proposals must be sought and considered. Their perspectives must shape the final text.

Employ iterative drafting. At least two rounds of draft proposals should be released, with opportunities for public comment between rounds. Each iteration should incorporate feedback on the previous one.

Safeguard independence of the Commission. The Commission must be protected from political interference. Its members must be free to exercise judgement based on analysis of public input and expert knowledge, not on partisan considerations.

Invest in civic education and communication. Citizens must understand draft proposals and how to engage with them. Communication must be sustained throughout Phase III, using multiple channels and accessible formats.

14.16 CONCLUSION

Phase III of Botswana's constitutional review is the bridge between consultation and decision-making. International best practice demonstrates that analysis, clustering, drafting and public engagement must be transparent, inclusive and iterative. By adopting these principles, Botswana can produce a constitution that reflects the aspirations of its people and strengthens democratic legitimacy.

Phase III is where the voice of the people is translated into the language of constitutional law. It is a technical task, requiring rigorous methodology and analytical skill. Still, it is also a deeply political task, requiring judgement about what the people have said and what it means for the constitutional text.

The stakes are high. If Phase III is done well, the resulting constitution will reflect the aspirations of the people and command their allegiance. If it is done poorly, the legitimacy generated through earlier phases will be squandered. The people will feel that their input was ignored, that the process was a sham, and that the constitution is just another elite document.

Botswana has an opportunity to get it right. By adopting transparent methodologies, ensuring inclusivity, employing iterative drafting, safeguarding independence, and investing in communication, the Commission can ensure that Phase III fulfils its promise. The result will be a constitution that the people truly own, that reflects their values and aspirations, and that can endure for generations.

RECAP AND TRANSITION

Recap: This chapter has examined Phase III of constitutional review: analysis, drafting, and further public engagement. It has explored the analytical foundations of coding submissions into thematic categories. It has examined the process of clustering themes and identifying both convergences and divergences, emphasising the importance of attending to minority voices. It has discussed drafting revision proposals, including the option of presenting multiple models for public debate. It has emphasised the importance of continued public engagement in Phase III, testing drafts through town halls, surveys, and digital platforms. It has examined international best practices of transparency, inclusivity, and iterative drafting. It has identified challenges and risks—political capture, public fatigue, managing divergences—and proposed safeguards. It has drawn on comparative case studies from South Africa, Kenya, and Bolivia to illustrate best practices. It has concluded with recommendations for

Botswana: adopt transparent methodologies, ensure inclusivity, employ iterative drafting, safeguard independence, and invest in civic education and communication.

Transition: Having analysed public input and developed draft proposals, the next chapter turns to the technical craft of putting those proposals into constitutional language. Chapter Fifteen examines **The Importance of Drafting**. It explores why drafting matters, how to choose drafters, how to ensure that drafters do not subvert the people's will, the value of plain language, and the risks and dangers inherent in the drafting process. Drafting is where the people's aspirations are finally fixed in constitutional text; getting it right is essential to the success of the entire enterprise.

CHAPTER FIFTEEN

THE IMPORTANCE OF DRAFTING IN CONSTITUTIONAL MAKING AND REFORM

15.1 INTRODUCTION

The constitution is a body of rules and maxims in accordance with which the powers of sovereignty are habitually exercised.

A constitution is a system of fundamental laws for the governance and administration of a nation. It is supreme, imperious, absolute, and unalterable, except by the authority from which it emanates. It has been defined as the fundamental and paramount law of the nation. It prescribes the permanent framework of a system of government, assigns to the different departments their respective powers and duties, and establishes certain fixed principles on which government is founded. The fundamental conception, in other words, is that it is a supreme law to which all other laws must conform and in accordance with which all private rights must be determined and all public authority administered.

Constitutional drafting lies at the heart of every nation's democratic journey. Whether creating a new state, rebuilding after conflict, or reforming outdated structures, the process of writing a constitution reflects both the identity and aspirations of a people. A constitution is not simply a legal document: it is a political covenant, a social compact, and a moral guide for governance. As the Constitution-Making and Reform: Options for the Process underscores, the legitimacy of a constitution depends not only on what it contains but also on how it is made.

Drafting, therefore, is more than a technical exercise; it is the process through which abstract ideals are transformed into legal text, principles into enforceable norms, and collective hopes into constitutional language. The success or failure of a constitution often hinges on how well this drafting process is managed—its inclusivity, transparency, and sensitivity to context.

This chapter explores the importance of drafting in the constitutional-making or revision process, focusing on five critical dimensions: (a) the importance of drafting itself; (b) the careful selection of drafters; (c) the necessity of ensuring that drafters do not subvert the people's will; (d) the value of using plain, accessible language; and (e) the risks and dangers inherent in the process. The discussion draws upon the experiences of the Philippines, Papua New Guinea, Bolivia, South Africa, Kenya, and Namibia, as well as insights from International IDEA (2011) and the United States Institute of Peace's Participatory and Inclusive Constitution-Making Processes (USIP, 2011).

15.2 THE IMPORTANCE OF DRAFTING

The drafting stage is the constitutional moment where vision meets precision. It determines whether the people's aspirations are faithfully captured in clear, just and implementable provisions. Good drafting fosters political stability, guides judicial interpretation and secures public confidence in governance. Conversely, poor drafting breeds ambiguity, litigation and mistrust.

In the drafting of the constitution, the structure of the government is clearly outlined. The rights of every citizen, which should be written in a form and style easily understood by them, are laid out, and it reveals the ideals and principles of the nation. The drafting of the constitution also serves as the basis for the formulation of laws to be implemented, observed and obeyed.

Constitutional drafting also ensures legal stability and continuity because the rules and principles on the operation of the government are determined, the qualifications of public key officials are set, the rules on succession are set, and the scope or limitations in the exercise of powers are delineated. The Constitution embodies the values and aspirations of a nation. It is an instrument that showcases what it stands for and encapsulates the inspiration of the people in the present time and for more generations to come.

One advantage of a written, conventional, and rigid constitution is its permanence, or its capacity to resist capricious or whimsical change dictated not by legitimate needs but only by passing fancies, temporary passions, or occasional infatuations of the people with ideas or personalities. "A constitution must be firm and immovable, like a mountain amidst the strife of storms or a rock in the ocean amidst the raging of the waves. Such a constitution is not likely to be easily tampered with to suit political expediency, personal ambitions, or ill-advised agitation for change."

As International IDEA (2011) emphasises, constitutional legitimacy arises not merely from formal adoption, but from public ownership of both process and text. The constitution must, therefore, be written in a way that reflects the people's values and political culture. The South African experience after apartheid illustrates this point vividly. The Interim Constitution of 1993 was the product of intense negotiations that ensured representation of diverse racial and political groups. Its successor, the 1996 Constitution, consolidated those compromises into a document renowned for clarity, inclusiveness, and human rights protection.

Similarly, the 1987 Constitution of the Philippines, drafted after the fall of authoritarian rule, served as a moral and legal renewal. The Commission, chaired by Cecilia Muñoz-Palma, sought to institutionalise democracy, protect human rights, and prevent the re-emergence of dictatorship. The deliberate drafting of safeguards—such as term limits, the Bill of Rights and the separation of powers—illustrates how careful wording can translate national trauma into structural reform.

In essence, drafting matters because it shapes how power is distributed and constrained. It also signals national identity and vision. In Kenya, the

2010 Constitution emerged from long years of struggle and consultation, culminating in a document that recognised devolution and diversity. These examples affirm that drafting is the arena where politics, law and morality converge.

15.3 CHOOSING THE DRAFTERS

Drafting the constitution is an important task that requires a clear understanding of society's needs to ensure the welfare of the people. The complexities of writing its provisions to translate not only the rights of the people and the enactment of laws, policies or regulations to protect such rights, but also to prevent abuse of rights, must be factored in. Many legal, political and social factors have to be properly weighed in so as to reflect the will of the people. Drafting likewise includes defining and limiting powers which are sought to be distributed among the branches of the government and safeguarding the same to prevent abuse of authority and corruption. Thus, the drafter is tasked to ensure that the provisions of the constitution are easily understandable by the ordinary people, being the source of their rights and the basis of laws to be enacted.

In this regard, the drafters must have the necessary skills, qualifications and experience in order to produce a constitution that embodies the best interests of the people. For one, the diverse cultural, religious and social groups in the different parts of the country should be represented because a constitution should be a written instrument that unites all the people within a nation. The youth should also have a voice in the drafting process because they are an essential part of the continuity of the nation. The freshness and openness of their views or perspectives contribute to innovation, which is fundamental to the progress of the country. The voice of the youth in this era of technological advancements can offer solutions to the challenges of evolving modernity. With their involvement in the drafting of the constitution, the constitution can become more responsive and adaptive to the present and future challenges, guaranteeing flexibility and continuity.

Along the same lines, a drafter must have a deep understanding of citizens' behaviour in society, governance, law-making, and law enforcement, as well as political science, because these elements shape how a nation works. The drafters must exercise ethical judgement and patriotism, upholding democratic values over personal or political gain. The process for selecting those who will draft the constitution must be transparent to ensure fairness.

The integrity of a constitution depends largely on the integrity of those who write it. Selecting competent, impartial and representative drafters is thus essential. Inclusivity in drafting promotes legitimacy, while exclusion fosters alienation and resistance.

In South Africa, the Constitutional Assembly was broadly representative, composed of parliamentarians elected in the first democratic elections. This ensured that all major political parties had a voice. In contrast, Papua New Guinea's Constitutional Planning Committee in the 1970s included traditional leaders and academics, allowing customary values to shape modern governance structures. The resulting constitution balanced Western democratic principles with Melanesian consensus-based traditions.

The Bolivian experience under President Evo Morales, who took power in 2006, highlights both the promise and peril of choosing drafters. The Constituent Assembly was composed mainly of indigenous and grassroots representatives (groups historically excluded from power). This broadened participation, but also created political tension with elites who feared radical change.

For the Philippines, the 1986 Constitutional Commission was appointed rather than elected, which drew some criticism. Yet, its members included lawyers, priests, academics, and activists, reflecting diverse sectors.

The Commission's success lay in its ability to work transparently and conscientiously despite political pressures. These comparative experiences show that choosing drafters is a delicate balance between expertise and representation.

15.4 ENSURING THAT DRAFTERS DO NOT SUBVERT THE WILL OF THE PEOPLE

One of the most significant risks in constitution-making is that those tasked with writing the document may shape it to serve their own or their faction's interests. To prevent this, robust mechanisms for participation, transparency, and accountability must be built into the process.

In keeping with the duty to draft a constitution that protects the rights of the people and promotes their common good, the process of drafting the constitution must be inclusive and encourage public participation.

Public participation bridges the gap between the government and the people. The involvement of persons who represent the different groups of society ensures that their needs and values are considered and valued. Allowing the public to participate in drafting the constitution will make them feel they are not mere subjects of government decisions, as their participation will enable them to voice what they genuinely need and ensure that their interests are valued. Relative thereto, there must also be persons tasked with monitoring the drafting process to ensure that no manipulation has occurred. Those persons should guarantee fairness to the masses and should not protect only a specific group.

Participatory constitution-making requires that the people are engaged not only in ratification but throughout the process. Mechanisms such as public consultations, civil society submissions, and publication of draft texts allow citizens to monitor and influence the drafters. In Kenya's 2010 constitutional process, the Committee of Experts organised nationwide forums and incorporated thousands of public submissions. This approach helped restore trust after the failed 2005 draft and ensured that the final text reflected broad consensus.

Namibia's Constituent Assembly (1990) also set a precedent for transparency. It operated under clear procedural rules and open debates, ensuring that the constitution reflected the independence struggle's ideals rather than party dominance. Similarly, in the Philippines, the 1986 Commission held public hearings and broadcast plenary sessions, a rare move that encouraged citizen involvement and scrutiny.

To further ensure fidelity to the people's will, a ratification mechanism, typically a national referendum, is indispensable. This final act reaffirms popular sovereignty. South Africa's Constitutional Court even reviewed the 1996 Constitution for compliance with agreed constitutional principles before certification, serving as a legal safeguard against subversion. Such innovations demonstrate that people's participation is both a right and a safeguard in constitution-making.

15.5 USING PLAIN ENGLISH

A constitution belongs to the people, not to lawyers alone. Its language should therefore be clear, precise and accessible. The use of plain English, or plain language in any national tongue, ensures that citizens understand their rights and the limits of state power.

Technical jargon, legalistic phrasing and archaic expressions alienate the public and allow manipulation by elites. International IDEA (2011) advocates for clarity as a democratic principle: "Language should empower, not mystify." The South African and Kenyan constitutions are commendable for their simplicity and readability, employing terms understandable to ordinary citizens.

In the Philippines, the 1987 Constitution used straightforward English, supplemented by Filipino translations for civic education. Public understanding of basic provisions—such as the Bill of Rights or the role of local government—has enhanced citizens' sense of ownership. In Papua New Guinea, the drafting committee consciously integrated Pidgin English terms and explanations during consultations, bridging linguistic divides and cultural nuances.

Clarity is not simplicity alone; it is precision with accessibility. The aim is to prevent ambiguity without diluting meaning. As legal scholar Justice Holmes once remarked, "The life of the law has not been logic; it has been experience." Hence, constitutional language must speak to experience, not merely to theory. Plain English promotes transparency, facilitates civic education, and strengthens the bond between citizen and constitution.

To add, the drafters should make sure that the constitution is broad, not only because it provides for the organisation of the entire government and covers all persons and things within the territory of the State, but more so because it is supposed to embody the past, to reflect the present, and to anticipate the future. The constitution must be comprehensive enough to provide for every contingency. It has been said that the constitution is "not only the imprisonment of the past but the unfolding of the future," to which it may be added that it is also the fulfilment of the present. It must be brief and confine it to basic principles, implemented with legislative details more adjustable to change and easier to amend. The constitution must be clear or definite, lest ambiguity in its provisions result in confusion and divisiveness among the people, and perhaps even physical conflict.

15.6 RISKS AND DANGERS

Despite its noble aims, the drafting process carries serious risks. The first is elite capture, where political or economic elites dominate deliberations to preserve their privileges. Bolivia's early constitutional debates revealed how entrenched interests can polarise society. Similarly, the Philippines' attempts to amend the 1987 Constitution have often been clouded by suspicions of self-serving political motives.

Another risk is haste and external pressure. In post-conflict or transitional contexts, the urgency to adopt a new constitution may compromise deliberation. Namibia's 1990 process was successful largely because it balanced speed with consultation, but many other nations have failed under international or political deadlines.

A third danger is exclusion. When women, minorities, or indigenous peoples are left out of drafting, the resulting document lacks legitimacy. The Kenyan and Bolivian cases show that inclusion enriches both content and acceptance.

Finally, ambiguity and poor drafting quality can undermine constitutional stability. Vague provisions may invite judicial confusion or political exploitation. The lesson from comparative experiences is that technical expertise must complement political participation. A constitution written in haste or confusion may sow future crises instead of resolving past ones.

15.7 CONCLUSION

Drafting a constitution is both a technical and moral act: an endeavour where words determine the fate of nations. It is in the drafting stage that justice is either institutionalised or deferred, and democracy is either deepened or diluted. The cases of the Philippines, Papua New Guinea, Bolivia, South Africa, Kenya, and Namibia reveal that successful constitution-making depends not merely on inspiration but on process: who drafts, how they draft, and whether the people's voice resonates in every line.

The drafters' task is sacred. They are entrusted not to author their own legacy, but to give voice to a nation's collective will. The use of plain, accessible language ensures that the constitution belongs to the people it governs. Yet, the process remains vulnerable to subversion, exclusion, and elite manipulation. For this reason, vigilance, participation, and transparency must guide every constitutional moment.

Ultimately, constitutional drafting is not just the act of writing law—it is the act of writing history. Its success lies in fidelity to the people's ideals and in humility before their sovereignty.

RECAP AND TRANSITION

Recap: This chapter has examined the importance of drafting in constitutional making and reform. It has explored why drafting matters: it is where vision meets precision, where the people's aspirations are translated into enforceable law. It has examined the critical task of choosing drafters, who must possess skills, qualifications, experience, and represent the diversity of the nation. It has addressed the risk that drafters may subvert the people's will, emphasising the need for participation, transparency, and ratification mechanisms as safeguards. It has advocated for the use of plain, accessible language, ensuring that the constitution belongs to all citizens, not just lawyers and elites. And it has identified the risks and dangers inherent in drafting (elite capture, haste, exclusion, ambiguity), and the importance of mitigating them through careful process design.

Transition: Having translated the people's aspirations into a draft constitution through careful analysis and drafting, the next chapter turns to the final phase of the constitutional review process. Chapter Sixteen examines **Phase IV: Final Adoption and Post-Adoption Education**. It explores international best practices in constitutional adoption, including parliamentary approval, judicial certification, and referenda. It recommends an optimal pathway for Botswana, combining parliamentary adoption, judicial certification, and a referendum to ensure both institutional legitimacy and democratic participation. It also emphasises the critical importance of post-adoption civic education to ensure that the new constitution is not only adopted but also understood, respected, and lived by the people.

Chapter Sixteen

PHASE FOUR – FINAL ADOPTION AND POST-ADOPTION EDUCATION

16.1 INTRODUCTION

Phase IV of the review process—adoption and ratification—is decisive. It determines whether the new constitution will be perceived as legitimate, whether it will endure political contestation, and whether it will command respect across generations. Adoption mechanisms vary globally, but they generally involve parliamentary approval, judicial certification, and/or direct public endorsement through a referendum. Each pathway carries distinct advantages and risks.

This Chapter situates Botswana's Phase IV within international best practice, drawing lessons from South Africa, Kenya and Bolivia. It explores the merits of parliamentary adoption, judicial certification and referenda, and recommends an optimal pathway for Botswana. Finally, it emphasises the necessity of post-adoption civic education to ensure that the constitution is not only legally binding but also socially embedded.

The adoption phase is the culmination of everything that has come before. The political mandate has been secured, the legal framework established, and the Commission appointed. Civic education has prepared the people. Consultations have gathered their views. Analysis has transformed those views into structured options. Drafting has produced a constitutional text. Now, the question is: how does that text become the supreme law of the land?

The answer matters enormously. A constitution adopted through a process that is perceived as illegitimate will struggle for acceptance, no matter how well-drafted its provisions. A constitution adopted through a process that commands broad confidence will enjoy the allegiance of the people, even if its provisions are imperfect. The mechanism of adoption is not merely a procedural formality; it is integral to constitutional legitimacy.

16.2 INTERNATIONAL BEST PRACTICES IN CONSTITUTIONAL ADOPTION

16.2.1 South Africa: Judicial Certification as Legitimacy Anchor

South Africa's 1996 constitutional process is often hailed as a gold standard. After years of negotiation, the Constitutional Assembly produced a draft constitution. However, adoption was contingent upon certification by the Constitutional Court. The Court assessed whether the draft complied with 34 constitutional principles agreed upon during the transition from apartheid.

This certification process had several implications:

- It ensured that the constitution was consistent with democratic norms.
- It provided legal credibility, reducing the risk of future constitutional challenges.
- It substituted for a referendum by embedding legitimacy in judicial authority.

South Africa's case demonstrates that judicial certification can serve as a powerful safeguard, especially in societies transitioning from authoritarianism to democracy. However, it also reveals the limits of elite-driven processes: while legally sound, the absence of a referendum meant that legitimacy rested heavily on institutional trust rather than direct public endorsement.

South Africa's innovation was to make adoption contingent on judicial certification. The Constitutional Court did not draft the constitution; it reviewed what the Constitutional Assembly had produced. Its task was to ensure compliance with 34 principles that had been agreed upon during the transition. These principles covered fundamental rights, separation of powers, democracy, and other essential features of constitutional government.

The certification process served multiple functions. It ensured that the final constitution was consistent with democratic norms, providing a safeguard against backsliding. It gave legal credibility to the document, reducing the risk of future constitutional challenges. And it substituted for a referendum, embedding legitimacy in the authority of the Court rather than in direct popular vote.

But this approach also had limitations. Legitimacy rested heavily on institutional trust: trust in the Court, trust in the political process, trust in the elites who had negotiated the settlement. In a society emerging from decades of authoritarian rule, that trust was not universally shared. The absence of a referendum meant that citizens did not have the opportunity to directly endorse their new constitution.

16.2.2 Kenya: Referendum as Democratic Legitimacy

Kenya's 2010 constitutional reform followed decades of political contestation. The process culminated in a national referendum, where citizens directly voted on the draft constitution. The referendum was preceded by extensive civic education campaigns, spearheaded by civil society and government institutions.

Key lessons from Kenya include:

- A referendum provides democratic legitimacy by allowing citizens to endorse the constitution.
- Civic education is indispensable to ensure informed participation.
- Public endorsement strengthens the constitution's durability, making it harder for future governments to undermine it.

Kenya's experience highlights the importance of public buy-in, particularly in societies with histories of exclusion and contested governance.

Kenya's approach was different from South Africa's. Instead of judicial certification, Kenya chose a national referendum. Citizens voted directly on the draft constitution, expressing their consent or rejection at the ballot box. This direct endorsement provided democratic legitimacy of a kind that no elite process could match.

The referendum was preceded by extensive civic education. Citizens needed to understand what they were voting on—the contents of the constitution, the implications of its provisions, and the arguments for and against. Civil society and government institutions collaborated to provide this education, using multiple channels and accessible formats.

The result was a constitution that commanded broad public support. This support has made it harder for subsequent governments to undermine the constitution. Any attempt to do so would face not just legal obstacles, but popular resistance.

16.2.3 Bolivia: Hybrid Pathway of Parliamentary Adoption and Referendum

Bolivia's 2009 constitutional reform combined parliamentary adoption with a referendum. The draft constitution was first passed by the legislature, then subjected to a national referendum. This dual pathway ensured both institutional legitimacy and democratic endorsement.

Bolivia also invested heavily in civic education, particularly in rural and indigenous communities. This outreach was crucial in a diverse society where constitutional reform sought to address historical inequalities.

Bolivia's case demonstrates that hybrid pathways can balance institutional rigour with democratic participation, while civic education ensures inclusivity.

Bolivia's approach combined the strengths of both models. Parliamentary adoption ensured that elected representatives had thoroughly considered the constitution and that it reflected the compromises and negotiations of the political process. The referendum ensured that citizens had the final say, that the constitution was not just an elite pact, but a popular charter.

The investment in civic education was critical. Bolivia is a diverse society with significant indigenous populations and deep historical inequalities. Ensuring that all citizens understood the constitution and could participate meaningfully in the referendum required sustained effort, particularly in rural and indigenous communities.

16.3 BOTSWANA'S PHASE FOUR PATHWAY

Botswana's constitutional review process must balance three imperatives: institutional legitimacy, legal soundness, and democratic participation. A proposed pathway for Phase IV includes:

1. **Parliamentary Adoption**
    - A two-thirds threshold ensures broad political consensus.
    - It anchors the constitution within Botswana's representative democracy.
    - It prevents narrow partisan adoption, which could undermine legitimacy.
2. **Certification by Constitutional Court**
    - Judicial review guarantees compliance with constitutional principles.
    - Certification enhances credibility and protects against unconstitutional provisions.
    - It provides an authoritative safeguard against political manipulation.
3. **Referendum Option**
    - A referendum provides direct democratic legitimacy.
    - It ensures public endorsement, strengthening durability.

    - It complements parliamentary and judicial adoption by embedding popular sovereignty.

Botswana can design a pathway that learns from the experiences of others. A hybrid approach, combining all three elements (parliamentary adoption, judicial certification, and a referendum), would provide the strongest foundation for legitimacy.

Parliamentary adoption with a two-thirds threshold ensures broad political consensus. It prevents a narrow majority from imposing its will on the nation. It anchors the constitution within Botswana's representative democracy, giving elected representatives a central role.

Certification by the Constitutional Court guarantees legal soundness. It ensures that the constitution complies with fundamental principles, that it does not contain provisions that are unconstitutional or unworkable. It provides an authoritative safeguard against political manipulation.

A referendum provides direct democratic legitimacy. It gives citizens the final say, ensuring that the constitution is not just an elite document, but a popular charter. It embeds popular sovereignty at the heart of the process.

16.4 COMPARATIVE ANALYSIS: CERTIFICATION VS REFERENDUM

Certification by Court

- **Advantages**
    - Ensures legal soundness and consistency.
    - Protects against unconstitutional provisions.
    - Provides authoritative validation by an independent institution.
- **Disadvantages**
    - Limited public participation.
    - Risk of judicial politicisation.
    - May be perceived as elitist or technocratic.

Referendum

- **Advantages**
  - Enhances democratic legitimacy.
  - Provides direct public endorsement.
  - Encourages civic engagement and constitutional literacy.
- **Disadvantages**
  - Costly and logistically demanding.
  - Risk of populism or misinformation campaigns.
  - Potential for divisive outcomes in polarised societies.

The comparative analysis reveals the trade-offs between certification and referendum. Certification ensures legal soundness but may be perceived as elitist. A referendum provides democratic legitimacy but carries risks of cost, misinformation and division.

The choice between them depends on context. In South Africa, coming out of apartheid, judicial certification provided a safeguard against backsliding and a substitute for a referendum that might have been divisive. In Kenya, with a history of contested elections and ethnic polarisation, a referendum provided direct public endorsement that no elite process could match.

Botswana's context is different from both. It has a strong tradition of institutional trust and political stability. It also has a history of elite-driven constitutionalism, with the 1966 Constitution adopted without popular participation. A hybrid approach, combining certification and referendum, would address both concerns: legal soundness through judicial review, democratic legitimacy through popular vote.

16.5 RECOMMENDATION

Botswana should adopt a **hybrid pathway** combining parliamentary adoption, judicial certification and referendum.

- **Parliamentary adoption** ensures institutional legitimacy.
- **Judicial certification** guarantees legal soundness.
- **Referendum** provides democratic legitimacy and public buy-in.

This three-layered approach balances institutional rigour with democratic participation. However, if resource constraints make a referendum impractical, Botswana could stop at judicial certification, provided that extensive public consultations and civic education campaigns are conducted. Conversely, skipping certification in favour of a referendum risks legal inconsistencies, which could undermine durability. Therefore, certification should not be omitted.

The recommendation is clear: a hybrid pathway combining all three elements. This approach maximises legitimacy across multiple dimensions. It ensures that the constitution is politically supported (parliamentary adoption), legally sound (judicial certification), and popularly endorsed (referendum).

The qualification regarding resource constraints is practical. Referenda are expensive. They require voter registration, polling stations, ballot papers, counting, and verification. If resources are limited, a choice may be necessary. In that case, judicial certification should be retained as it ensures legal soundness. Extensive public consultations and civic education can partially compensate for the absence of a referendum, though they cannot fully replicate its democratic legitimacy.

Skipping certification, however, is not advisable. Without judicial review, the constitution may contain legal inconsistencies or unconstitutional provisions. These could undermine its durability and lead to future challenges. Certification is a safeguard that should not be omitted.

16.6 POST-ADOPTION CIVIC EDUCATION

A constitution is only as strong as the public's understanding of it. Post-adoption civic education is essential to ensure that citizens are familiar with their rights and responsibilities.

Strategies for Botswana

- **Media Campaigns**: Radio, television, and social media to reach diverse audiences.
- **School Curricula**: Integrating constitutional literacy into education systems.
- **Community Dialogues**: Grassroots engagement through local leaders and civil society organisations.
- **Translation and Accessibility**: Ensuring the constitution is available in all major languages and formats, accessible to persons with disabilities.

The adoption of a constitution is not the end of the process; in many ways, it is the beginning. A constitution that sits on a shelf, unread and unknown, cannot shape the life of the nation. It must be brought to life through ongoing education and engagement.

Media campaigns can reach diverse audiences. Radio reaches remote rural communities. Television reaches urban populations. Social media engages youth. By using multiple channels, post-adoption civic education can ensure that all citizens learn about the new constitution.

School curricula integrate constitutional literacy into education systems. Children learn about the constitution from an early age, developing the knowledge and dispositions that sustain constitutional democracy. This is a long-term investment in constitutional maintenance.

Community dialogues provide opportunities for grassroots engagement. Local leaders and civil society organisations facilitate discussions, answering questions and addressing concerns. These dialogues deepen understanding and build ownership.

Translation and accessibility ensure that the constitution is available to all. Translations into all major languages make the text accessible to linguistic communities. Formats accessible to persons with disabilities, for example, Braille, audio, and large print, ensure that no one is excluded.

Lessons from Case Studies

- Kenya's civic education campaigns before the 2010 referendum significantly improved public understanding.
- Bolivia's grassroots outreach ensured that even marginalised communities were familiar with constitutional changes.
- South Africa's participatory drafting process created a sense of ownership that reduced the need for a referendum.

Kenya's experience demonstrates the value of sustained civic education. Campaigns before the referendum significantly improved public understanding, enabling informed participation. Bolivia's grassroots outreach ensured that even marginalised communities were familiar with constitutional changes, building ownership across diverse populations. South Africa's participatory drafting process created such a strong sense of ownership that a referendum was less necessary; citizens felt they had already been part of the process.

16.7 CONCLUSION

Phase IV of Botswana's constitutional review process is pivotal. Adoption pathways must balance institutional legitimacy, legal soundness, and democratic participation. International best practices suggest that a combination of parliamentary adoption, judicial certification, and a referendum provides the most robust framework.

Botswana should prioritise a high parliamentary threshold, certification by the Constitutional Court, and, if feasible, a referendum to secure public endorsement. Post-adoption civic education is indispensable to ensure that the new constitution is not only adopted, but also understood, respected, and lived by citizens.

Ultimately, constitutional literacy is the foundation of democratic resilience. By embedding it into Phase IV, Botswana can ensure that its new constitution is not merely a legal document, but a living covenant between the state and its people.

The adoption phase is the culmination of the constitutional review process, but it is also the beginning of the constitution's life. The document that emerges from Phase IV will shape Botswana's governance for generations. Its legitimacy will depend on the process that produced it. Its endurance will depend on the understanding and commitment of the people who live under it.

By adopting a hybrid pathway—parliamentary adoption, judicial certification, and referendum—Botswana can maximise legitimacy across multiple dimensions. Investing in post-adoption civic education, it can ensure that the constitution is not just adopted but lived. The result will be a constitution that commands allegiance, that shapes behaviour, that endures through crises and changes.

This is the goal of the entire constitutional review process: not just a new document, but a renewed constitutional order, grounded in the will of the people and capable of guiding the nation into the future.

RECAP AND TRANSITION

Recap: This chapter has examined Phase IV of constitutional review: final adoption and post-adoption education. It has explored international best practices, drawing on South Africa's judicial certification model, Kenya's referendum model, and Bolivia's hybrid approach. It has proposed a hybrid pathway for Botswana combining parliamentary adoption (with a two-thirds threshold), certification by the Constitutional Court, and a referendum. It has analysed the advantages and disadvantages of certification versus referendum. It has emphasised the critical importance of post-adoption civic education, recommending strategies including media campaigns, school curricula, community dialogues, and translation into accessible formats. It has been concluded that constitutional literacy is the foundation of democratic resilience, and that embedding it into Phase IV ensures that the new constitution is not merely adopted but lived.

Transition: Having traced the entire constitutional review process—from preliminary questions through preparation, consultation, analysis, drafting and adoption—the next chapter brings the manuscript to a close. Chapter Seventeen provides a **Conclusion** that summarises the entire manuscript, synthesising the key themes of both Part 1 and Part 2. It reflects on the relationship between constitutional foundations and review processes, the importance of constitutional literacy, and the path forward for Botswana's constitutional democracy.

Chapter Seventeen

CONCLUSION – SUMMARY

17.1 INTRODUCTION

This book has journeyed through the foundations of Botswana's constitutional order and the process by which that order may be reviewed and renewed. Part One examined the historical origins, philosophical underpinnings, structural features and rights-protecting mechanisms of the Constitution of Botswana. Part Two explored the principles, phases and practices of constitutional review, drawing on comparative experience to chart a path forward for Botswana.

This book has been written in simple and plain English to introduce readers to the idea of constitution, republicanism, and the process of reviewing a constitution. By design, the pages of this book are brief. This is meant to facilitate interest in reading the book and absorbing its content faster. It is hoped that this booklet will promote and enhance constitutional literacy and an understanding of how government works in a constitutional democracy.

The journey has been guided by a central conviction: that constitutions derive their authority not only from legal validity but from popular ownership and participation. As argued in this book, a constitution that is technically sound but born through exclusion, secrecy, or elite bargaining may struggle for legitimacy, compliance and endurance. The process by which a constitution is made is as important as the content it contains.

This conclusion draws together the threads of the manuscript, summarising the key findings of Part One and Part Two, reflecting on the relationship between constitutional foundations and review processes, and offering final reflections on the path forward for Botswana's constitutional democracy.

17.2 PART ONE: FOUNDATIONS OF THE CONSTITUTION OF BOTSWANA

Part One of this book established the foundations upon which any constitutional review must build. It began with the historical origins of Botswana's Constitution, tracing its journey from the Lancaster House Conference and Lobatse talks to its adoption at independence in 1966. As Chapter One explained, Botswana's Constitution emerged through consultation rather than conflict, moving from Lancaster House negotiations, through local Lobatse discussions, to a carefully crafted independence constitution in 1966. This foundation has contributed significantly to Botswana's long-term political stability. However, the people were not involved in its design and creation. In many respects, it was a colonial imposition or elitist at best.

This legitimacy deficit at the founding moment has animated much of the subsequent discussion. Chapter Two explored the philosophical foundations of popular sovereignty and the social contract, drawing on the political philosophy of John Locke. It explained why sovereign people need government, how government is formed through consent, and what obligations government and citizens owe each other under the social contract. The idea of "*We the People*" as sovereign lies at the heart of Botswana's constitutional democracy. While sovereignty belongs to the people, government is necessary to secure rights, maintain order, and promote collective well-being.

Chapter Three examined what it means for Botswana to be a sovereign republic. It explored the principles of republicanism, representative government, and electoral systems. Botswana's constitutional democracy is grounded in republicanism and representative government. Its written constitution enshrines the nation's status as a republic and guarantees fundamental rights. Botswana's electoral system—First Past-The-Post—has helped sustain political stability and accountability, but also presents challenges concerning proportional representation and inclusiveness.

Chapter Four examined the framework of constitutional democracy itself. It explored constitutional government, constitutionalism, the rule of law, good governance, separation of powers, checks and balances, and the protection of human rights. Constitutional democracy in Botswana is founded on the supremacy of the Constitution, the rule of law, separation of powers, and protection of fundamental rights. While Botswana has achieved remarkable constitutional stability, continuous reflection and reform are necessary to respond to changing social needs.

Chapter Five provided a detailed examination of the Bill of Rights in Botswana's Constitution. It analysed each of Sections 3 to 18, explaining the content of each right, exploring judicial interpretations, and considering enforcement mechanisms. The Constitution of Botswana provides robust protection for fundamental human rights through the Bill of Rights enshrined in Chapter II. Sections 3–18 collectively safeguard individual freedoms, limit governmental power, and promote democratic values. Through judicial interpretation, particularly by the Court of Appeal, these rights have been given practical meaning and enforceability.

Chapter Six explored the concept of constitutionalism—the principles and practices that ensure government power is exercised within constitutional limits. It distinguished constitutionalism from the mere existence of a constitution, examined its key components (rule of law, separation of powers, protection of rights, accountability, transparency, judicial review), and drew on scholarly perspectives from Locke, Montesquieu, Dicey, McIlwain, and Feldman. Constitutionalism is the soul of a constitutional order. It is what transforms a mere document into a living framework for limited, accountable government.

17.3 PART TWO: THE CONSTITUTIONAL REVIEW PROCESS

Part Two of this book turned from foundations to process. It began with an introductory chapter establishing why process matters as much as content. Drawing on the concept of conversational constitutionalism, it argued that constitution-making should be a sustained national conversation, not a one-off consultation. It emphasises dialogue over decree, listening over persuasion, and mutual learning between citizens and experts. Rather than viewing citizens as passive recipients of expert knowledge, conversational constitutionalism treats them as co-authors of constitutional meaning.

Chapter Eight addressed the preliminary questions that must be answered before any constitutional review process can begin. It examined whether a comprehensive review is needed, how law and politics interact in constitution-making, who should frame the roadmap, whether a stakeholder conference is required, who should draft the terms of reference, what a constitutional assembly is and how it should be composed, and what guidelines should govern the process. Comparative experience demonstrates that the way a constitution is made is often as important as its final content. Poorly designed processes risk elite capture, exclusion, and long-term instability, while inclusive and transparent processes can contribute to peacebuilding, national ownership, and democratic consolidation.

Chapter Nine examined the roles of civil society, political parties, and media in constitution-making. It explored how civil society can broaden participation, translate lived experience into constitutional language, provide expertise, and mediate conflict. It examined how political parties can forge inclusive settlements or undermine processes through domination. It examined how media, both traditional and digital, shape the information environment. Civil society, political parties, and media are not peripheral to constitution-making; they are central to its legitimacy.

Chapter Ten articulated guiding principles for an inclusive and participatory constitutional review process in Botswana. It set out principles of legitimacy, accessibility, inclusivity, transparency, public participation, accountability, independence, consensus-building, respect for human rights, evidence-based approach, timeliness, civic education, gender sensitivity, sustainability, and deliberation over polarisation. These principles are not abstract ideals but practical requirements for democratic governance and social cohesion. Ultimately, an inclusive and participatory constitutional review process strengthens not only the constitution itself but also the democratic culture upon which Botswana's future depends.

Chapter Eleven examined Phase I: Foundation and Preparation. It explored establishing a political mandate, enacting a Constitutional Review Act, creating an independent Constitutional Review Commission or Assembly, and conducting civic education. Comparative experience demonstrates that successful constitutional reform begins not with drafting, but with careful preparation. Phase I must therefore be approached as a foundational investment in legitimacy, trust, and democratic governance.

Chapter Twelve provided an in-depth examination of civic education, drawing on theoretical frameworks and comparative experiences. It explored civic education as an antidote to constitutional rot, reflective patriotism, education as a constitutional right, and civic education as constitutional maintenance. Civic education is not a luxury or an add-on; it is essential to constitutional legitimacy and endurance. Sustained investment in civic education builds the capacities and dispositions that constitutional democracy requires.

Chapter Thirteen examined Phase II: National Consultation and Public Participation. It explored multi-channel public submission (digital platforms, physical submissions, sectoral hearings), grassroots consultations (town halls, public hearings, focus group discussions, targeted methods for marginalised groups), and collection and synthesis (systematic data collection, thematic analysis, transparent reporting). Constitution-making is a complex, political, and inherently participatory process. The transparent publication of submissions, the presence of independent commissions with strong credibility, and consultations conducted across multiple platforms foster legitimacy and broad ownership.

Chapter Fourteen examined Phase III: Analysis, Drafting and Further Public Engagement. It explored coding submissions, clustering themes, identifying convergences and divergences, drafting revision proposals, and continued public engagement. International best practice demonstrates that analysis, clustering, drafting, and public engagement must be transparent, inclusive and iterative. By adopting these principles, Botswana can produce a constitution that reflects the aspirations of its people and strengthens democratic legitimacy.

Chapter Fifteen examined the importance of drafting. It explored why drafting matters, how to choose drafters, how to ensure that drafters do not subvert the people's will, the value of plain language, and the risks and dangers inherent in drafting. Drafting a constitution is both a technical and moral act—an endeavour where words determine the fate of nations. It is in the drafting stage that justice is either institutionalised or deferred, and democracy is either deepened or diluted.

Chapter Sixteen examined Phase IV: Final Adoption and Post-Adoption Education. It explored international best practices from South Africa, Kenya, and Bolivia. It recommended a hybrid pathway for Botswana, combining parliamentary adoption (with a two-thirds threshold), certification by the Constitutional Court, and a referendum. It emphasised the critical importance of post-adoption civic education. Ultimately, constitutional literacy is the foundation of democratic resilience. By embedding it into Phase IV, Botswana can ensure that its new constitution is not merely a legal document but a living covenant between the state and its people.

17.4 THE RELATIONSHIP BETWEEN FOUNDATIONS AND PROCESS

Throughout this book, a central theme has emerged: the intimate relationship between constitutional foundations and constitutional process. The foundations established in Part One—popular sovereignty, republicanism, constitutional democracy, the Bill of Rights, constitutionalism—provide the normative framework within which any review process must operate. The process examined in Part Two—preparation, consultation, analysis, drafting, adoption—determines whether those foundations will be renewed or eroded.

A constitution that is technically sound but born through exclusion, secrecy, or elite bargaining may struggle for legitimacy, compliance and endurance. This insight applies as much to constitutional review as to original constitution-making. A review process that is itself exclusionary or manipulated will produce a document that lacks legitimacy, no matter how progressive its provisions.

Conversely, a constitution that emerges from a participatory and inclusive process may command allegiance, even if its provisions are imperfect. The process itself educates, empowers and legitimises. It transforms subjects into citizens. It creates the conditions for constitutional endurance.

Botswana's 1966 Constitution, whatever its technical merits, was born without popular participation. This legitimacy deficit cannot be corrected solely by inserting progressive clauses; it must be addressed through a comprehensive and participatory review process.

17.5 THE CENTRALITY OF CONSTITUTIONAL LITERACY

Another theme that has run throughout this book is the centrality of constitutional literacy. The purpose of this book is to promote and enhance constitutional literacy and an understanding of how government works in a constitutional democracy.

Constitutional literacy is not merely knowledge of constitutional provisions. It is an understanding of constitutional principles: popular sovereignty, separation of powers, rule of law, and fundamental rights. It is the capacity to engage with constitutional issues, to deliberate with others, to hold government accountable. It is a commitment to constitutional values, to defending the constitution against erosion and attack.

Civic education is the primary mechanism for building constitutional literacy. As Chapter Thirteen explored, civic education operates as both the medium and the measure of democratic constitutionalism. The success of constitutional reform depends less on the elegance of institutional design than on the capacity of citizens to understand, internalise and defend the constitutional principles that govern them. Constitutionalism is sustained not by text alone, but by civic learning, reflective engagement, and institutional participation.

Constitutional literacy must begin before the review process and continue after it. It must be embedded in schools, media, community organisations, and public life. It must reach all citizens, in all languages and all locations. It must be sustained across generations.

17.6 THE PATH FORWARD FOR BOTSWANA

Botswana stands at a constitutional crossroads. The 1966 Constitution has served the nation well, providing stability and continuity for more than half a century. But the world has changed since independence. Understandings of human rights have deepened. Expectations of democratic participation have risen. New challenges have emerged that the framers could not have anticipated.

The demand for constitutional review reflects these changes. As Chapter One noted, there is an apparent yearning amongst Batswana to create a modern constitution that could be a normative statement against authoritarianism. For this aspiration, there is a need for political will and a strong civic culture rooted in the values of transparency, accountability, inclusivity, and fairness.

The path forward requires commitment to the principles articulated in this book: legitimacy, accessibility, inclusivity, transparency, public participation, accountability, independence, consensus-building, respect for human rights, evidence-based approach, timeliness, civic education, gender sensitivity, sustainability, and deliberation over polarisation.

The path forward requires careful attention to each phase of the review process: foundation and preparation, civic education, consultation, analysis, drafting, and adoption. Each phase must be designed and implemented with the same care that goes into constitutional drafting itself.

The path forward requires learning from comparative experience. South Africa, Kenya, Bolivia, Namibia and others offer lessons in what works and what does not. Botswana can adapt these lessons to its own context, building on its strengths while addressing its challenges.

17.7 FINAL REFLECTIONS: THE CONSTITUTION AS LIVING COVENANT

A constitution is more than a legal document. It is a political covenant, a social compact, a moral guide for governance. It embodies the values and aspirations of a nation. It shapes how power is exercised, how rights are protected, and how conflicts are resolved. It binds current and future generations in a shared project of self-governance.

For a constitution to fulfil these functions, it must be more than technically sound. It must be legitimately born. The people must own it. It must be understood and defended by citizens. It must be lived, not just cited.

This is the goal of constitutional review: not just a new document, but a renewed constitutional order. A constitution that reflects the will of the people. A constitution that responds to lived realities. A constitution that offers fair rules for political competition. A constitution that can endure through crises and changes.

Botswana has a historic opportunity. The constitutional review process, if designed and implemented according to the principles and practices outlined in this book, can deepen democracy, strengthen national unity, and produce a constitution for the twenty-first century. The journey will not be easy. It will require political will, resources, patience, and commitment. But the destination is worth the effort: a constitution that the people truly own, that commands their allegiance, that can guide the nation into the future.

Ultimately, constitutional literacy is the foundation of democratic resilience. By embedding it into every phase of the review process and into the ongoing life of the constitutional order, Botswana can ensure that its constitution is not merely a legal document, but a living covenant between the state and its people.

RECAP

Recap of the Entire Book: This concluding chapter has summarised the key themes of both Part One and Part Two of the book. Part One examined the foundations of Botswana's constitutional order: its historical origins in the Lancaster House Conference and Lobatse talks; its philosophical underpinnings in popular sovereignty and social contract; its republican character and electoral system; its framework of constitutional democracy, including separation of powers, checks and balances, and the rule of law; its Bill of Rights protecting fundamental freedoms; and its commitment to constitutionalism as the soul of constitutional government. Part Two examined the process of constitutional review: why process matters as much as content; the preliminary questions that must be answered before review begins; the roles of civil society, political parties, and media; the guiding principles for an inclusive and participatory process; the four phases of review:

1. foundation and preparation; 2. civic education; 3. consultation, analysis and drafting, and adoption; and 4. the critical importance of post-adoption civic education. The chapter has reflected on the relationship between foundations and process, the centrality of constitutional literacy, and the path forward for Botswana. It has concluded with final reflections on the constitution as a living covenant between the state and its people.

www.ingramcontent.com/pod-product-compliance
Lightning Source LLC
LaVergne TN
LVHW090316210926
848480LV00001B/262
* 9 7 9 8 9 0 3 6 2 3 2 1 1 *